THE DONNA GENTILE STORY

The Life and Murder of an Innocent Runaway

San Diego's NHI Murder Victom

THE DONNA GENTILE STORY

The Life and Murder of an Innocent Runaway

San Diego's NHI Murder Victom

Anita DeFrancesco

Rosey PUBLISHING

PROJECT CREDITS

Cover & Book Layout: www.freezetimemedia.com

Cover Design Illustration Artist: Jonathan Borowko

NHI Photo Artists: Deborah Small, Scott Kessler, Elizabeth Sisco, Carla Kirkwood, & Louis Hock

Library of Congress Catalog Card Number: 2018960024

ISBN 978-0-9822616-1-3

This book is dedicated

To all the Voiceless Women of the World....

May Your Voice Be Heard

In Memory of My First Cousin

Donna Gentile

August 22, 1962 - June 23, 1985

Philadelphia/San Diego, California

DONNA means "Lady" and GENTILE means "Gentle"

To all the "Gentle Ladies" of the world...

honor your feminine nature and never let go...

It's Your Voice

it's your voice

making me sing so fine

hearing your call

and I'm generous like God

you've owned me

a hundred times

buy me once more

give me a new life

RUMI

Contents

Foreword

"The Donna Gentile Story" is a true crime story. It is the true crime story of my first cousin and friend, Donna Gentile, 22 years old, found dead, murdered. Like so many others, her story ends as an unsolved mystery, otherwise known as a cold case.

What's different is that this murder still baffles the San Diego community as to what, who, how, and why it happened. That city should know the full details of this story as should we. The murder of Donna Gentile was nationally publicized — it hit every newspaper from the "San Diego Tribune" to the "Los Angeles Times," the "New York Times" and the "Pennsylvania Bucks Courier Times." To me it was a story of a prostitute who stood up for her rights. Her actions reflected the "MeToo" movement of today. She paid with her life.

This book does not convict, condemn, or blame anyone, nor am I trying to prove anything. I have compiled the details of Donna's life and the events leading up to her murder. I have gathered information from public documents, interviews, news sources, family and a YouTube documentary created by Professor Jerry Kathleen Limberg of Cal State focusing on Donna's death, prostitution, and the underlying relationship of both with the San Diego Police Department. Early on, in 1993, my journey took me to Norma Jean Almodovar, former LAPD officer and author of "Cop to Call Girl." This gave me a greater understanding on the subject of policing and prostitution. She founded the International Sex Worker Foundation for Art, Culture & Education in Los Angeles and is the director of Coyote. I later met Dr. Annie Sprinkle, a sex-positive feminist who founded the "International Day to End Violence Against Sex Workers" memorial, which takes

5

place annually on Dec. 17, along with the Sex Workers Outreach Project, USA in 2003. I also connected with Melanie Dante, an advocate of the project who campaigns and leads the event in Philadelphia. She further enlightened me on the topic of police, prostitution and women killed. I am telling the story in the way I believe Donna would have wanted it told.

Donna's life is a story of betrayal, abandonment, voicelessness from a young age, not heard. And so Donna becomes a runaway, the typical choice of young girls that are unheard, abandoned, and devoid of love.

And so, how does one survive as a runaway? Prostitution. But more than prostitution for Donna Gentile. So much more ... she is coerced. She is exploited to serve the San Diego Police Department, Internal Affairs. From there, her death.

While I was living in Los Angeles, Donna would often come to mind. I was drawn to visit San Diego. It was a two-hour drive. As I drove, a dark cloud would come over me, a somber fear pierced me, but most of all I felt a presence, the presence of Donna. I trembled. I visited Mt. Laguna where Donna's body was found. The image of Donna flooded my mind. I felt her terror.

Lying there, dead, pebbles in her mouth. Was that Donna's dream? No. She dreamt of love, family, home, the white picket fence, the dream of so many young women of her day.

Did Donna choose prostitution? No, prostitution chose Donna. It was an iron fist. A fist born of pain, abandonment, and despair. And then, cast off ... voiceless, and at the end, lying down, dead ... pebbles stuffed in her mouth.

Disclaimer

This book is drawn from a compilation of public documents, personal interviews, news sources, family and a YouTube documentary on the relationships between Donna Gentile, her death, prostitution, and the SDPD.

I have made every effort to ensure that the information presented here is correct. This book is presented for informational and entertainment purposes only. While my best efforts have been used in preparing this book, neither the author nor the publisher offer its content as evidence of crime, nor as a complete and accurate historical record.

Neither the author nor the publisher shall be held liable or responsible to any person or entity with respect to any loss or incidental or consequential damages caused, or alleged to have been caused, directly or indirectly by the information presented here.

1

The Beginning At The End

A young woman's body was discovered off of Sunrise Highway 30 miles east of San Diego County, in Mt. Laguna, set in the forest surrounded by Jeffrey pine, which sits 6,000 feet above sea level. The high point of this scenic drive extends from Interstate 8 to Highway 79. It was Sunday, June 23, 1985, a sunny, summer day in America's best climate state. The medical examiner would later report that she had died a day earlier. She was found naked, and her body had been beaten and strangled. Gravel was stuffed down her throat.

Donna's murder scene in this ravine.

The woman was Donna Gentile, and her killer or killers are still at large today. No murder is routine or inconsequential. Family and friends must face the shock of losing a loved one, and it can take years to move on from the event. Sometimes, moving on is impossible. It is especially difficult when law enforcement never apprehends the killers.

When you throw in the added component that the local San Diego police, the very people who are supposed to "Serve and Protect," could be complicit in the crime, the scars from such a terrible event encourage the family doing whatever they can to help solve the mystery.

That is one of the missions of this book. As the cousin of Donna Gentile, I want justice administered. At the least, I want to clearly state who Donna was, the events in her life that led to her premature death, and the series of events that went on after her death to impede and sidetrack any real investigation of her murder.

After almost 35 years, there is always hope that the truth will see the light of day. It becomes more difficult as time goes on, but by laying out a systematic telling of Donna's life and the activities of the San Diego Police Department at that time, one can determine logical possibilities of who might be Donna's murderers. If our efforts lead current law enforcement to investigate her case more vigorously, then it was well worth the effort to assemble this book using over thirty years of collected facts and clues.

Donna Gentile was from Philadelphia and moved west after dealing with issues at home. Settling in San Diego, she became a prostitute to make ends meet and survive. Due to her role as a prostitute, she became a police corruption informant for the cops in San Diego. Weeks after giving testimony in a highly-publicized hearing against two officers for engaging in improper conduct with a prostitute, she was found murdered.

The San Diego County Medical Examiner determined that Donna was alive when her killer pushed gravel down her throat. This is a common method of marking a murder victim as a "snitch." Furthermore, the area where the sheriff's department found the body appeared to be carefully brushed clean of any tire marks, footprints, or any other clues. The area was a carefully calculated and orchestrated placing of the girl's body rather than a random murder and dumping.

As you will see, Donna was making efforts to leave her prostitute's life behind and could have been successful if she didn't get mixed up with the San Diego Police Department. At that time, corruption and cops doing anything they wanted filled the department. They exercised their power, especially over prostitutes. The cops would target and use them for sex in exchange for keeping them out of jail. Donna had been charged and convicted several times on prostitution charges and, eventually, became entangled with two cops in particular: officer Larry Avrech and Lieutenant Carl Black. Her life became further complicated when the Internal Affairs division of the police department recruited her as a police corruption informant.

I have pulled the details of Donna's life and the events leading up to her murder from public documents, interviews with people of interest, news sources, family and a YouTube video focusing on Donna's death and the relationship between prostitution and the San Diego Police Department between 1980 – 1993. All sources and acknowledgments are in the appendix of the book.

Each chapter of the book will focus on one aspect of Donna's life or the open murder case. And, yes, it is still open. A report as recent as May 22, 2017, by CBS 8 in San Diego, puts the murder of Donna in perspective and is why we feel this book is necessary:

Prostitute Donna Gentile's autopsy will remain sealed, even though it's been more than 30 years since the police informant's high-profile murder.

Gentile, 22, was found naked, beaten and strangled off Sunrise Highway in 1985, five weeks after she implicated two San Diego Police officers in a prostitution scandal.

Reports that the killer had stuffed gravel in Gentile's mouth led some to wonder if she was murdered because she talked.

In her May 1985 testimony before the Civil Service Commission, Gentile alleged that SDPD officer Larry Avrech had been to her apartment on several occasions, and that the two had sexual contact. Avrech, at the time age 32, denied having sex with Gentile but he was fired from the police department nonetheless for giving Gentile inside information on vice raids.

Gentile also testified about traveling to the Colorado River with SDPD Lieutenant Carl Black and other SDPD officers. Black was demoted to sergeant for contacting Gentile's probation officer on her behalf.

In December 2015, CBS News 8 requested the San Diego County Medical Examiner release Gentile's autopsy under the California Public Records Act. The agency issued a denial letter, which said the San Diego County Sheriff's Department wants to keep the autopsy sealed:

Until this directive is rescinded by the investigating agency, we are unable to release any information or provide any copies of our reports regarding this case... The public interest in the release of these reports and the information contained within does not outweigh the public's interest to withhold this information as it may interfere with law enforcement's investigation and/ or a successful prosecution.

The question naturally arises about what information could possibly interfere with "law enforcement's investigation and/or a successful prosecution." As far as anybody knows, there has been no official work done on the case for some time. From an outside observer, it seems that the autopsy and other official facts of the case are being kept under wraps to protect someone. You cannot help but figure that law enforcement is protecting law enforcement.

I will systematically lay out all the information on the events and people leading up to Donna's murder. The sad truth here is that no matter where this might lead, it will not bring Donna back to her family. However, the other purpose of this book is to be a message for other young girls out there who might find themselves going into a similar lifestyle as Donna.

Donna had the potential to make a better life. She was a talented, articulate woman. She was smart and knew she didn't want to live the life of a prostitute for much longer. In fact, she was taking steps to grow in a different career. She was working as a security guard with aspirations of working in law enforcement. This was a particular irony when it was her association with law enforcement that ended her life. She had also met someone who wanted to marry her and take her back to the East Coast.

As we explore Donna's early life, you can see how easily a girl might end up on a path of prostitution. When a girl finds herself out on her own with no means of support, it is an easy path to choose. Sex for money or some other compensation has been around forever. It is certainly nothing new, and today in 2018, the means to exercise that lifestyle are easier to access than it was in 1985. Cell phones, social media, and the means to advertise make it as easy for a woman to sell her body for sex as it is to find a job or look for an apartment.

It doesn't matter if a girl advertises on craigslist or hangs out on a street corner. The point is that these young women are people who see prostitution as a means to an end. For some, it simply means keeping a roof over their head and food on the table. Some women take this road to pay for college and move on to a career. Others get caught in a downward spiral of drugs and criminals. Some disappear. Others end up dead like Donna.

When it comes to prostitution, it is sad that the police and public opinion treat prostitutes that end up in prison or worse as if their lives didn't matter because of what they did. That is the furthest thing from the truth! All lives matter no matter what their path.

"When one woman is violated, it is a powerful threat to all women"

Anita

At the end of the book, we talk about organizations that are out there to help empower women regardless of what they are doing or have done.

I hope that this book gives a voice to Donna. I cannot but wonder what her life would be like now if it weren't cut so short. If this book reaches one girl or the family of a girl who has turned to prostitution, and it helps her life to change, then Donna would be happy. Likewise, if it helps people realize why young women can fall into prostitution and what that kind of life can be like, then it will help humanize those women. When you realize that a hooker is a real person who has all the same hopes and fears as everybody else, then it is the beginning of a positive change in attitudes towards those that have to go that route.

Finally, this book is a modern-day parable of what can happen to those we put into power to protect us. The job of law enforcement is to protect all people, even street prostitutes. To them, prostitutes are part of the underclass, and because of this labeling they are considered expendable and classified as NHI. "NHI" stands for "No Humans Involved." This is a despicable term that law enforcement sometimes used to describe victims of a crime who were on the outer edges of society. Cops didn't think they needed to go out of their way to protect people like prostitutes, the homeless, or other fringe members of society. As we have seen in recent events, this attitude can also extend to differences in gender, race, sexual orientation, etc. Furthermore, not only is protection towards NHIs lax, but so is the effort to investigate any crimes where they are victims, even murder.

For a prostitute, especially one at the mercy of the San Diego Police Department in the 1980s, life is fragile. Being a prostitute is one thing, but being sexually harassed by a police officer to sleep with you is another. This was a widespread practice in San Diego, and the odds are good that it led to Donna's death. Donna looked

to police for protection, but in the end, it was her undoing.

We want to make the point here that not all cops, even those in the San Diego Police Department in 1985, are corrupt. However, as you progress through Donna's story, you will see that it was an institutional problem in the city's police force at that time and had a direct bearing on the tragic events at the end of her life. We often wonder what craziness possessed Internal Affairs to coerce Donna to become a police informant to report on corrupt cops. It seems like it all goes back to prostitutes being thought of as something less than a person.

I was at the center of this whole drama that filled our family with tears, fears, and worry. I still remember that hot sunny day in June sitting in the living room of our South Philadelphia home. It was around noon, and I was eating lunch and talking to Mom. There were loud noises outside of children playing ball, trash trucks driving by, and cars honking. Then this surprisingly loud knock hit the door. Two tall, serious-looking men in suits identified themselves as San Diego detectives. When they broke the tragic news to Donna's brother, who had been living with us, we were shattered, frozen, and in shock. I immediately broke into a cold sweat, and my mother was speechless. Brother Lou was sitting with his head down and just taking it all in. Donna was a family member, and that's all that mattered. She was one of us. From her letters of fear, we knew anything was possible. We were numb and filled with frozen tears that would continue to build as pain and anger over time.

This was June 1985, and they were investigating the murder of my cousin, Donna Marie Gentile. Brother Lou was 24, and I was 28. Our 20s are the most precious and scarring and can shape our lives forward forever. The detectives spoke with us for a while, filling us in on all the details, collecting letters and information from us. Donna is still very much alive to us. I can still feel her vibrancy and her pain. It is the pain and vibrancy of all women who are treated unfairly and suffer. Tragedies that touch our lives are the hardest, but the best teacher we can have.

This book discusses an entangled true crime. It is also very personal. I have laid out Donna's life and her time in San Diego based on the facts and insight I have available. She was only 22. So many girls are just finishing college and heading out on their own at that point. Donna had lived a lifetime by then. We know she was getting her life together and then the triangle of friendship, sex, and politics within the San Diego Police Department came into play.

My family has been kept in the dark for the last 30 years as to who murdered Donna. Here is her story. See what you think.

2

A Girl's Life

Donna's story was one of light and darkness, and patterns repeating themselves. Our family was like so many others where the sins of the past intruded into the lives of the children. This did happen to Donna, and it led to her ending up in San Diego and living a life that concluded with someone killing her. Donna's story is profound and can be inspiring to girls and women who want to uncover hidden strengths and find resiliency to face whatever demons are in their life. We know that she found inner peace before she met her end.

It was August 22, 1962, a hot summer day in North Philadelphia, when a beautiful baby girl named Donna Marie Gentile was born to Ellen Mary and Louis Francis. Louis was my mother's brother and, therefore, my uncle. Both Ellen and Louis grew up in Philadelphia. Donna's two parents had their city in common, they were both Catholic, and they both had alcoholic fathers while growing up.

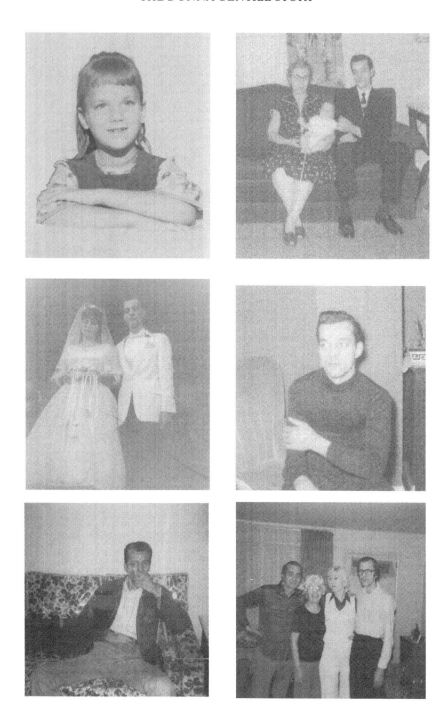

Left page, clockwise from top left: Baby Donna;, Grandmom, Donna, Lou Sr;
Lou Sr.; Tony, Grandmom, Roseanne, Lou Sr.; Lou Sr.; wedding of Ellen & Lou
Sr.

This page, left to right: Donna & Grandmom, Lou Sr.

Alcoholism is never easy for family members. Back in the '50s and '60s, there were not many programs for dealing with it and virtually no support system for the affected family. According to what my mother alleged, Ellen's father was overtaken by alcohol more often than not. He emotionally abused her and unleashed a great deal of negativity towards her. He tried to control her and deprived her of her rights as a child. He demonstrated very antisocial behavior toward his daughter and other family members. Her father did not like the men she brought home, including Louis.

According to my mother, Lou's father would come home and lock Lou's sisters in the bedroom without supper. On some occasions, the father would fall flat on his face on the living room floor and lie there drunk for hours. Lou Sr. was afraid of his father, due to his actions, and this led to Louis becoming emotionally unstable and neurotic. When children are exposed to helpless parents with emotional challenges, there is a transference that sets in and is passed on in the genes. Transference is the redirection of feelings and desires, especially of those unconsciously retained from childhood. Both Ellen and Lou experienced unconscious transference that later manifested in their children.

Lou and Ellen became codependent particularly because of the pain they endured in their upbringings. Dysfunctional childhoods often cause the kids to become unstable and make poor choices in life as an adult. Ellen was always looking for the man of her dreams. Lou was both in love and obsessed with her. Ellen and Lou would go to the drive-in movies back then when making out and having sex was the thing to do. Ellen became pregnant at 18 with Lou Jr. She left home and married Louis, who was ten years older than her. Ellen seemed to be in search of that father figure that women so often trap themselves into doing.

This is all setting the stage for when Donna was born two years after Louis Jr. As all babies are when they are born, Donna was an innocent. She wanted love and compassion as all children do. However, Donna was born to parents who had emotional challenges from the start. They wanted to be good parents for their children, but their love wasn't strong enough to keep them together. Ellen and Lou were troubled young teens who weren't ready to have children or even to be married, for that matter.

What ended up happening is that Donna would grow into a troubled teen herself. It was one of those patterns that develop in families. My aunt and uncle were average people who did their best in trying to raise her and her brother, Lou Jr. Children only know the life they experience, and by the time Donna was born, there wasn't much love in the home. If you don't receive love, it's hard to know how to give it. Because Donna's parents were troubled, they carried this into their lives with the children.

As time passed, Aunt Ellen studied to be a practical nurse and Lou became a cook at a restaurant. Lou and Ellen worked together and tried to make their marriage last. Their relationship was one of pain, jealousy, obsession, domestic violence, and possessiveness. According to my mother, Donna witnessed the physical abuse that went on between her parents. This leaves a child with fear and mental scars. My aunt and uncle would have huge battles, split up for a while, and then get back together again. For my two cousins, it was a constant emotional roller coaster at home.

My relationship with my cousin Donna was simply one of first cousins getting together to visit. Her father and my mother were sister and brother. My mother had a strong relationship with Louis, Donna's father, and reached out to help her brother as often as she could. I still remember that when we were kids, our families would visit together.

They lived in northeast Philadelphia, and I still remember the wide-open house with the bow window where the light would always shine into the home. There were the kitchen and back door where we would go on the lawn while the adults conversed. I remember Uncle Louie would be very helpful around the house and Aunt Ellen would tend to the children. They were cigarette smokers. Aunt Ellen was a beautiful woman who would always be conscious of her appearance. I knew why my uncle obsessed over her; her beauty was stunning.

I was eight years older than Donna, and I adored my

little cousin. We would play like kids do, out on the lawn and in the living room. I remember Donna as a little girl, and the memories endured of when I used to pick her up and shower her with hugs and kisses. She was very cute, and I didn't realize until much later how that constant turmoil in the house affected the innocent little girl I played with in the yard. Because of all the mean talk she heard between her mother and father, and the constant splitting up, Donna had to feel abandoned and unloved. She could only wish for a harmonious togetherness that didn't exist there.

Donna expressed her unhappiness with the family, but it fell on deaf ears. You learn happiness from happy people. It's contagious. As a little girl, Donna just wanted to live a normal life and would say how she wished her parents would not fight so much. Children can only blossom when there is security, love, and trust. The lack of it was just the beginning of her pain and dysfunction. Children are very creative, and sometimes a voice comes in that is stronger than them and their parents.

Children long to come from a secure, loving family. When that isn't there, they can become unstable and have emotional challenges later on in life. The atmosphere in her childhood was devoid of love and Donna experienced a painful journey from the very beginning to the very end. Emotional patterns of pain, frustration, and poor decisions became a reoccurring pattern for Donna. She deserved love and attention like any other child, but her parents were not able to provide it in a healthy, balanced way. She became frozen to what was going on in her surroundings. Donna's parents lived a great deal of emotional pain between them. Parents in this state sometimes become numb to their feelings and neglect their children in ways that they are not aware is happening.

Ellen and Lou stayed together as long as they could. Ellen

just wanted to be away from her father and had rushed to marry Lou. Donna was repressed and endured a lot of pain and suffering watching her parents argue. She was a scared little girl who became fearful of her surroundings. She lived in fear each day, never really knowing when love was going to show up. When Donna approached age nine, her life went from dysfunctional to fractured as her parents divorced. Uncle Lou was 41 when they divorced in 1971. Her brother Lou was just 11.

The one strong relationship that Donna had in her life was the bond she had with her brother Lou. Nothing could sever that, and it was often the saving grace that she clung to throughout her short life. Without the love and the bond with her brother, she might not have survived as long as she did or accomplished anything. Family was an important part of Donna's life.

Even today, Lou still holds that space for her. When Lou and Donna separated, they kept in touch. They talked as often as possible, and she wrote and called him frequently when she eventually moved to San Diego. She wanted him to move there with her. She wanted to keep the closeness with her brother alive in her life. Louis was all she had. I witnessed her letters and calls to her brother regularly. These two people could bond and care for each other very well. I remember wishing back then that I could have that type of bond with my siblings.

After her parents divorced, Donna and her brother were split up. The last time Lou Jr. and Donna saw each other was in a courtroom when the parents were arguing visitation rights. He went with his father, and she went with her mother. Ellen moved on with Donna. Ellen and Lou Jr. didn't see eye to eye, so he went with his father. We believe that Ellen had her suspicions about Lou Sr, and she didn't want her daughter near him. Aunt Ellen denied Donna her visitation rights with her father. Essentially, it was also the last time she came in contact with her father.

By being split up from Lou Jr., Donna left the only person she received any love from in her life. This separation created a dark shadow in Donna's life. Ellen moved Donna around as her mother sought a new husband. Ellen's childhood dysfunction always had her looking for that special man that would take care of her and keep her out of harm's way. If she found that person, she would do anything for him.

Because of Ellen's unsettledness, Donna moved through a succession of school systems and apartment complexes in Philadelphia and Bucks County, Penn. This was when Donna was between the ages of 10 and 17. She was 11 when they settled in Bucks County, outside of Philadelphia. They lived in apartments in Penndel, Middletown, Falls Township, and in Pennsbury. She attended four schools including Our Lady of Grace School in Penndel and Christ the King School in Northeast Philadelphia. For a young girl who had no foundation of family, love, support, or even a place to live, Donna's early life was more reminiscent of a traveling gypsy family than a typical family of the 1970s.

Our Lady of Grace School

Christ the King School

Ellen finally found a man whom she fell in love with and they married. Donna, Ellen, and her new husband became a family and moved to Levittown, Pennsylvania. Donna was 15 at the time.

Levittown was a baby boomer suburb and an up-and-coming part of Bucks County. The Levitt brothers constructed the area from 1951 to 1957. It was the white American Dream because they didn't sell homes to African-Americans then. This planned suburban community was soon the largest suburb of Philadelphia. This is where Donna found herself, and it seemed that

she could begin to put down roots and have some stability in her teenage years.

Unfortunately, darkness hit Donna's life again. According to family accusations, letters and news sources, Donna alleged there was inappropriate sexual advances during the first week of her new home life and that's why she ran away. Her words: "I just freaked out." Unfortunately, Ellen, Donna's mother, did not believe her and had no idea of what really was the problem. Women back then did not have the character of strength to stand up for themselves. Essentially mothers in this position subconsciously and unknowingly set their daughters up for their future. Almost at the same time, Donna's father died.

Donna's mother did not step up at all. First, she kept Louis' death from Donna, because she didn't want to upset her family life with her new husband. Ellen and Donna weren't any different than other mothers and daughters. They argued and were in disbelief with each other. It was the typical mother and daughter fights that went on. Ellen did not want to rock the boat at home and did the best she could to keep things smooth. Although her mom had good intentions of providing well for Donna, she had so much more to learn about love and life. Back then, the times didn't support women and emotions. The world kept women on a shameful, narrow ridge that did not allow for personal evolution.

You have to remember that back in the '70s women did not have the independence we see now. It was a time in our country when women hadn't connected as a whole, at least not in the greater Philadelphia area. For many women, being able to live decently meant you had to have a husband in your life. As mentioned earlier, Ellen was always looking for that special man. Now that she believed she found it in this man , she didn't want to lose him. It was easy to be in denial that Donna was only making up stories. When a child isn't acknowledged and believed by a parent, their lives can be devastating, and the revenge they want to take out on the parent generally is turned inward and manifested in their own self-sabotage.

Her daughter did manage to attend one school in Philadelphia for three straight years before moving to Levittown. Then she became a high school dropout. Donna was very intelligent, but everything up to the point to her new homelife finally sent her off the edge. A spokesperson at her school said about Donna after her death, "She was an average kid with average grades who drifted through life." Donna had episodes of running away, drinking, and missing school. She was staying out all night with girlfriends and hung out with bad people. When the alternative is going home to a disheartened situation there is not much choice.

The new life Ellen coveted was not good for her daughter. Donna didn't have any support or supervision, so what was she to do? Kids are resourceful. Donna had a choice of running away from it or tolerating the challenges at home. She collected her strength and confined her early exploits to running away locally.

Levittown and the surrounding area had horse tracks and stables. When Donna began to run away, she would go to these stables and find happiness and solace in the horses. Her brother Lou worked at the Bensalem Race Track grooming horses with our Uncle Frank DiVincenzo. Bensalem Race Track has since merged with the Parx Casino. Lou and Donna's mutual love of horses was one of those things that fueled their strong bond together. To them, it seemed that horses were the divine, the path to enlightenment. This is where she found love and strength for herself. Some people find strength in a doll or an object. Others do so with an animal, which is what occurred for both Donna and Lou.

Remember that Lou lived with his father while Donna was with her mother. This was a period where brother and sister had little contact. When Louis Sr. died of a stroke on June 7, 1977, he was only 46 years old, so the death was unexpected. According to my mother, Aunt Ellen allegedly did not allow Donna to attend her father's funeral. Donna's mother kept her father's death from her as well as the Social Security checks sent to Donna as a result of the death. It would become an issue between them that continued when Donna fled to San Diego. Aunt Ellen like many parents unknowingly project and displace their own personal pain onto their children. As I see it, on some subconscious level, mothers in this position hate their children for ruining their life. Wounded mothers can fall into this category and children are left feeling abandoned. However, the mother or child is not the blame. It is the collective energy of the world.

Donna never even got to go to her dad's funeral and never received a thing from Social Security. I can only feel compassion and sadness for Donna for all she went through at such an impressionable age. A person's middle teenage years are difficult under the best circumstances. Struggling with losing her father already compounded a screwed-up home life.

When her father died, Donna would continue to live with her mother and her new husband. My mom and her three sisters came together to figure out where Lou would go. The final decision was that my mother, Roseann Gentile DeFrancesco, would become Lou Jr.'s legal guardian and he would come live with us. It was 1977 when Lou Jr. came to live in our South Philadelphia home with me, my sister, and my two brothers. My mother had been divorced, and this was certainly a struggle for her financially.

I was just 20 and already helping mom care for the family after our dad left. Cousin Lou was 17 and a minor. We loved having him with us, but he was a teenager, and teenagers are always a challenge. He made new friends on our street, and everyone engaged him as a brother. Donna was always on his mind, as well as his mother and her life and his deceased dad. I could only wonder what went through his head and the pain he was carrying around. We showed him love and support.

Life at home for Donna was coming to a head. Her parents tried to discipline her, which was probably the best thing they could do considering the circumstances. Donna was such a troubled teen and ran away so often that her parents thought it best to put her in the Tabor Home for Children, which was a home for delinquent children in Doylestown, Penn. It was 1978 when she began to live there for at least two years. They put her in that home to give her a

My mom, Roseanne Gentile DeFrancesco.

chance at finding a stable life. In the end, this is where Donna and a girlfriend escaped from, boarded a bus, and headed to San Diego.

After the day in the courtroom at the divorce hearing when they last saw each other, the bond between Donna and brother Lou was strong until the day she died. They were very tight as brother and sister. Even though they never physically came into contact again, they continued talking through phone calls and letters. In fact, my adult relationship with Donna came through her brother, who had been living with us at the time of her life in San Diego. He shared her letters, phone calls, and Christmas cards with us, and conversations with cousin Lou were always full of good words about his sister. She would call at least three times a week. I could see that he cared and loved her. He constantly worried about her, which considering the life she had to lead at times, is understandable.

We were trying to keep our lives above water as best that we could. I admired the closeness he had with his sister. On several occasions, my mother and I encouraged Lou to ask Donna to come home. At one point, we began putting our thoughts together as to where she would live. We were a big part of this whole thing from the time she left until her death. Essentially Donna and Lou were like my siblings since my mother took care of Lou as his legal guardian. She wanted to see her brother's children happy and secure after he passed away. She became a mother to cousin Lou and encouraged him to find a more solid path in life. He ended up joining the Navy, and then married Pam in 1993 and had a son, Anthony, in 1995. Lou also continued working with the horses at Bensalem race track; it was the spirit magic of the horse that kept him connected with his sister. However, we couldn't get to Donna. She had a path of her own. I've learned that we all must navigate our own path. It is our own unique journey where we find ourselves. Lou had close relationships with grandmothers on both sides of the family, which fulfilled the bond of love for him.

When children don't receive a balanced love in the family, they can experience an emptiness inside and seek out ways to fill the void. In some cases, it's drugs. In Donna's life, her substitute for love was getting into a car with a man. The saving grace was that Donna had a strong, loving relationship with her brother from the time she was a child, but their early separation kept her searching and seeking that elusive *something*.

You can see that Donna's upbringing was anything but stable; she was a troubled teen without direction. Her fractured childhood caused the instability that plagued her life. There was an effort to sustain a direction, but it was clouded with gray. Her growing pains were tougher than for most children. Inside, she was just a hurt little girl with no real aim or structure. Children experience anger and sadness when exposed to instability, and they can become neurotic and fall in with the wrong circle of friends, as Donna did. What was admirable about Donna was that she sought to save herself in any way that she could.

3

Tabor Home Escape

It was 1980, and Donna was 17. The Tabor Home was where Donna lived when she escaped her way to California on a bus with a girlfriend. It was the last place she occupied in Philadelphia for approximately two years. The location of the Tabor Home for Children was in the suburbs of Bucks County in Doylestown, Penn. The grounds spanned over 96 wooded acres at the Fretz mansion estate. Thomas Cernea was the architect who developed the center.

The Tabor home dates back to 1907 when Mrs. Emma Chidester approached Rev. Philip Lamartine of the Tabor Evangelical Lutheran Church in Philadelphia. He accepted her visionary offer to open a home for destitute children. By 1913, "The Women's Board of Managers of the Tabor Home for Children" was organized.

The home trained Sisters of the Lutheran Deaconesses of the Mary J. Drexel Home of Philadelphia to provide care and stability so that children could build character and self-respect along with nourishing their mind and soul. This was the grass-roots philosophy that brought the home into existence.

By the 1920s, the home was open to boys and girls and new dormitories built. They took pride in keeping up with health and sanitation. The trustees received many donations and grants from the state to enhance and continually develop this home. There were 20 auxiliary women on the board who represented eleven churches surrounding the Philadelphia area. In June 1934, the Women's Board paid off the mortgage.

Tabor Home

Donna resisted going to this place. She fought with her mom and stepdad about this. She tried to escape on several occasions. However, Donna was a minor and didn't have a choice. She was controlled in many ways by her parents because they did want a stable upbringing for her, but they couldn't do it with the dysfunctional elements that challenged their psyches. At least, they were smart enough to seek out help. She was then sent to a facility that represented order and control. She was a child not allowed to blossom into her own person since the normal family life didn't exist for her and that is where children grow unconditionally. Children need freedom within structure. Perhaps that's why she escaped to a place like San Diego where the air, the weather, and the environment were as free as one can get.

This home was a lonely place for Donna as no family member visited. We just knew she was there. Perhaps it was not open for visitors, but not even her brother saw her when confined to this institution. The institution was like a reform school; it represented discipline, control, and restriction. Donna became erratic and an unacceptable child to have around to her stepdad and mother. They thought it would be best for her there. It was run by women and nuns when Donna arrived.

I'd like to say that Donna did get something out of her time at Tabor. When looking at her life in San Diego, you could see that she had to develop some organized, disciplined skills to keep her dreams alive. Perhaps she got her sovereign strength by living in this home that was pioneered by women.

While sending her to the Tabor House might have seemed like a good choice in one way, in another way it wasn't. To me, it was like dumping a child somewhere for someone else to raise. Donna wasn't any different from any other kid hanging on corners, drinking, etc. because of parents not giving them attention. The good thing is that the institution existed, and people had a place to go. I understand how a child would be resistant to confinement in an institution especially when you had a family. This was the beginning of Donna building that relationship with herself. I believe she clearly had a connection with a higher power, and she developed courage from the nuns that aided in her survival of the ups and downs of life to follow.

As time went on, the Tabor Home expanded its services and development. It constructed a swimming pool. They later hired full-time trained guidance counselors who had experience in psychiatric studies to provide more value to the children. By this point in the late '60s, the Commonwealth of Pennsylvania required all children to receive an education. Tabor had to regroup, refocus, and develop a more clearly defined policy. In 1974, they hired their first social worker. The social workers were instrumental in bringing the creative arts programs into play. They sustained the arts of music and crafts so that children could develop their talents. Tutoring was also on the uprise to enforce reading and math skills. Even today, it has a wide array of children's mental health services.

The home progressed into a full-time program utilizing staff, volunteers, and community resources. Recreation activities stressed cultural, educational, and recreational pursuits. By 1979, about the time when Donna escaped, it widened its spectrum of services and changed its name to Tabor Children's Services.

In 1978, when Donna started to live there, Tabor became nonsectarian, which meant they were evolving into a more secular organization. The amicable separation occurred between the Tabor Board of Trustees and the Lutheran Church. By 1979, a foster care program and independent living program were approved. In 1980, the state approved and licensed Tabor as an adoption agency. Perhaps if Donna stayed on board there, she might have been adopted or released back to her own family. One can only speculate as to why she wanted out of there. Maybe the talk of turning the place into an adoption agency scared her. Whatever the reason, Donna was free and on her way to San Diego.

The next chapter shows what a young runaway faces

when she travels cross-country to escape the loneliness and hell of her home or institutional life. It is a too common story with definite lessons to be learned. What surprises most people is how Donna survived and started to get a handle on her life until it was cut short.

4

Donna's New Life

L eaving the Tabor Reform Home was Donna's complete
break from the greater Philadelphia area and the life
she had there. This was in March 1980 and Donna was
seventeen years old. She and a girlfriend boarded a bus and
headed west. Their journey eventually ended in San Diego,
which means "Saint Didacus" in Spanish and is the birth-
place of California. After a while, her girlfriend went back to
Philly, but Donna stayed.
For the first time in a
long time, she finally felt
free. It was a happy time
for her to be out of the
mess at home and she
was excited by the
prospect of starting a
new life.

Since she was a child, she dreamed of living near the ocean, and this was one dream she attained. Early spring in San Diego is a great time of the year. Actually, the weather in San Diego is as close as you can get in the United States to perfect weather year-round. After the cold of Philadelphia, both regarding winter weather and her life at home and the Tabor Home, San Diego seemed like the Promised Land. Donna liked the people she met. She enjoyed walking around the city and the Pacific Coast beaches. As she navigated her way around this new city with the sun beating pleasantly on her face and hair, it hit her that she was alone and far away from home. Considering her predicament, she felt light-hearted for the first time in years and decided to stay when her friend left.

The predicament was that she was only 17. She was certainly old enough to make decisions. However, she had no skills of any type in order to find a job. She was of age to drive but had no car. She had a few dollars left in her pocket. No place to live. It was not going to be easy. She made steps to get off the streets.

Donna's story is one of survival and neglect. She certainly survived a lousy childhood and her early teen years. That was more of a case of just hanging on. She drew on her strength and helped herself in any way that she could. San Diego was an awakening for her. When she arrived in the city, she didn't know who she was. Within months, she discovered a part of herself that was unexpected. Donna found out that she could do whatever it took to live on her own. It wasn't always easy, and some might question her actions, but she managed to live, if not thrive, during the five years there before her death. Upon arrival in San Diego, she was searching for love, acceptance, and security, like any other girl her age. To some extent, she found all of that at times. She was definitely on an upward track when her life ended.

I always wondered what she would be doing now if she was still with us. For a lost soul with nowhere to go because she didn't receive much love at home, Donna discovered who she was and what she could accomplish.

Her first problem was money. She needed it to survive, and for a girl with no skills, that was going to be an issue. Her mother, Ellen, could have been a help here. Not by sending her any money that she and her husband had, but just by allowing Donna to have the Social Security checks that she was entitled to since her father passed away.

This was a problem since Donna was in Philadelphia. Ellen was getting the checks designated for Donna and cashing them. Whether she was rationalizing that they were to help pay for Donna's upbringing or putting the money away for Donna's future, we will never know. The fact is that once Donna was out of the house, the money should have gone to her. We aren't talking about a long time here. In August of 1980, Donna would turn 18, and the checks would stop. However, having money for those months could have taken her on a different path as she would have had some income to live on and maybe have a little time to figure out a different career path.

It is important to note that even with all the conflict with the money and the cumbersome homelife, Donna loved her mother. Sometimes the line was blurred between love and hate, but, for the most part, they stayed in friendly contact while Donna lived out west. Her mother had no idea she was a prostitute; it was only after her death that she found out about her lifestyle. Perhaps if her mother knew, she may have become closer to her daughter and reached out to rescue her, or continue to abandon her. Donna lived a paradoxical life. She loved the freedom to be on her own, but she still valued her family ties. This was especially true with her brother Louis, but she didn't cut off contact with her mother either. Donna seemed to have a sense that life was not black and white but was more like different shades of gray. She probably understood how her mother came to her point of view needing to side with her new husband. Donna didn't have to like it or live it anymore, but she could understand why Ellen lived as she did after splitting up from Louis, Sr. Letters and phone calls to her brother showcased her frustration with her mom, but that didn't mean she never wanted to see her again.

It seemed that the smooth, easy path didn't exist for Donna; she had to stand up for her rights constantly from a very young age. She certainly had to do this with her dysfunctional upbringing and was not believed or acknowledged. It was a rough childhood. The Social Security checks are another example. There would be much more fighting for her rights in the next five years as Donna had to constantly stand on her own two feet and push back against the world. Imagine that you're a young girl watching your friends with normal healthy families and you have to push and pull yourself through every moment just to exist as a human being. For a while she was homeless but she did all in her power to help herself and re-create her life.

Children in her shoes often become an adult sooner than they wish to because they must give up being a child. This is where a human split forms at a cellular level. Development stops, and it becomes noticeable as a numbness later on in life unless the individual seeks out the proper help. Fear takes over the body because of the abandonment they experience. To abandon is to withdraw one's support especially as it relates to responsibility and duty. The disconnection from a primary attachment triggers fears, and it becomes a pattern in which the individual functions. When parents abandon their children, the child feels unworthy of love and carves a path to find and complete that. Donna's early history provided her with this psychological character.

Donna did go to the Social Security office in San Diego but never could get the check matter straightened out. It wasn't a lot of money but living in 1980 was a lot different than it is now. Living was cheaper, and people didn't require as much as they do today. You didn't have to worry about having smartphones or a phone plan. The early home computers were just coming to the market, and the internet didn't exist. The money from Social Security could have provided the basics of food, shelter, and clothing for Donna and she would have had time to look for a job. She had no real skills at that time, but she probably would have found something.

So, you have a young girl who is ecstatic to be away from a family life that was slowly tormenting her. She was happy to be in sunshine and warmth. She probably had that feeling of shedding a 1,000-pound boulder off her shoulders. However, Donna was still a lost and lonely young girl. Her one friend quickly headed back to Philadelphia. Donna wanted her friend to stay since that was the only close connection she had. Donna had nobody to talk to about her feelings of anguish, rage, and terror. She was the kind of kid who wanted to be accepted. With no money, she did find a way to make a living as well as have a support group of sorts.

She fell into prostitution out of desperation. It was her choice. Young people make choices without direction or parental support. Mistakes happen. Not that she had too many options. The point is that she went out and started doing it on her own. She didn't have a pimp. She went out on El Cajon Boulevard, San Diego's most famous area for guys to pick up streetwalkers for sex.

Whether it was to have a girl hop in a car to give a guy oral sex, or go somewhere for more, men had their choice on El Cajon Boulevard.

The boulevard is a major east-west thoroughfare through San Diego, La Mesa, and El Cajon, California. Before the creation of Interstate 8, it was the principal automobile route from San Diego to El Cajon, the Imperial Valley and points east as U.S. Route 80.

El Cajon

Again, this was very reflective of the 1980s. Today, prostitution is as big as it ever has been. However, it is often done more subtly. With the internet, women easily advertise what they offer. There are websites grouped by specialty. Many young women finance college or even law or medical school by hooking up with a wealthy sugar daddy or two. Forty years ago, every major city had their areas known for prostitution. Many still exist today, but it isn't as prevalent as back then. About the only way a new prostitute could sell herself was by being seen. Many girls hoped they could build up a steady clientele, so they could at least stop walking the streets.

Donna had a lot going for her that helped her in her new

line of work. First, she was a pretty girl. She was going to get a guy's attention when she walked by, let alone attracting someone who was looking to pay for sex. She was intelligent and well-spoken. She was classy and clean. Donna was not a drug addict; however, she explored the drug culture at that age like any other teenager. She kept a good head on her shoulders. She didn't work for a pimp or anything like that. She was her own person.

Most men who are looking to pay for sex want someone exactly like Donna. On some level, they want to like the girl they are with and want someone who is sane, pretty, and clean. If they are pleasant to talk with, then all the better. Sometimes these men even rescued these girls like in the movie "Pretty Woman" where Julia Roberts played the hooker rescued by a client.

This was the life that Donna started on. It wasn't something she did steady for her five years in San Diego. It was a big part of her life, and it was something that she went back to when other work fell through. It was not something she enjoyed doing. In phone calls and letters to her brother, she would tell him what she was doing. She would point out that it was a matter of survival quite often; not something she wanted to do.

I still remember the feeling I embodied when I heard she was homeless. Chills and fears moved up and down my spine. This tragedy was a catalyst that helped me solidify my trajectory and carve out my career direction. I wanted to help women and men find the answers as to why these things happen and why men seek out prostitutes. Psychology and sex education is where I landed. It just made me want to run out there, hold Donna, give her the compassion she needed, and rescue her.

Donna used her charm and people skills in ways other than prostitution. She was very good at networking with people even before the term came into vogue. Now, some of the people she got to help her over the years in San Diego might have started out as clients, but Donna was a genuinely likable girl that people wanted to do things for when she asked. She was honest and outspoken, and her friends saw she had potential and was different. They knew that one day she would get rescued from the life.

For example, there was one man that she lived with for a while. He kept a roof over her head and gave her a secure place to live as she states in a letter. She liked it there, but after a bit of time, he started to push her to have sex. She was not attracted to him in that way. Sometimes a man feels entitled to a woman's body. Donna might have been a prostitute, but she had the same dreams of love and family that all young girls have. Besides, just because a girl is a prostitute doesn't mean anyone is entitled to have sex with her. She was a person with boundaries. She did want the fairytale ending at some point, but she knew she had a long way to go before she would find it. In regards to this guy, Donna did find a security job and saved up enough money to move out.

She worked for a few different security companies, including Triple and Timmins. Security companies were a step in the right direction of her procuring a police career one day. What Donna liked about working in security was she wore a uniform and a badge that gave her a sense of self-worth, well-being, and control. The job didn't require much education. Since she was a personable young woman, working and greeting people came naturally for her.

"I have a right to my body integrity"

Donna

She did manage to find places to live. At one point, she made enough money that she shared an apartment with a girlfriend. Unfortunately, she was arrested several times as a prostitute and spent a couple of days in jail here and there. As a repeat offender, her last jail stint was several months long, and the parents of a girlfriend took her in when she got out. She lived with them when her body was found.

To illustrate how prostitution was treated, here is the text from one of her first probation letters. The first arrest for prostitution is a misdemeanor, and San Diego offered community service time instead of jail. With more arrests, the repeat offenses become a felony with harder sentences. However, following her first arrest on January 21, 1981, her probation letter shows how relatively easy things were for Donna in the beginning.

From: County of San Diego

To: Donna Marie Gentile

Your case has been chosen for assignment to a new kind of caseload with less reporting in person to your probation officer.

Most of your reporting to your new probation officer will be by mail unless you are directed to report in some other manner. Enclosed is a supply of monthly report forms (406). You are expected to complete and submit one such form each month. When your supply of forms is reduced to one or two, please request additional forms from your officer. Even though you are reporting by mail (1) you must report any arrest to your Probation Officer within 24 hours, either by telephone or in person; (2) you must also report any change of address immediately by telephone, in person, or by mail.

You will still be expected to obey all the conditions of your probation, and your new Probation officer may order you to meet with him if he feels he needs to talk to you in person. If you have any problems or questions about your probation at any time, you may still talk to your probation officer on the telephone.

Your new Probation officer is S. Males
The telephone number is 236-5249

Very truly yours,
Cecil E. Steppe
Chief Probation Officer

(6-81)

Donna with her car and Bear

People liked Donna. She would use that quality to help herself in any way possible. She used to call her brother three times a week. Back in the day, it wasn't cheap to call long distance. Donna would give her brother a number and told him to reverse the charges. She had someone on her end in San Diego who would let her call him and pick up the cost. She would always check in with her brother with caring phone calls and letters. Back in June of 1981, she told him she still had her dog (Bear) and car and was living with a girlfriend and was receiving welfare until she got another job. Donna and her brother were very fond of each other.

One of her networking contacts helped Donna get that security job mentioned earlier. She had ideas of going into law enforcement and liked the idea of a security company. There was a relative in the family who had been a sheriff. Between that and all the cops Donna got to know in San Diego, becoming a cop would have been appealing. I think if Donna weren't killed, she would probably have ended up with a career working on a police force or going into some area of the law.

Donna and Bear

The security job would be a steady income with benefits. She wouldn't have to work the streets, and it was something she could be proud of doing. In fact, Donna sent her mother a photo of herself in her security uniform with a bright silver badge on her chest. There is obvious pride on her face. Teenagers want to prove themselves to a parent. Children are always looking for acknowledgment and acceptance. Donna was no different. She worked security for a while. Unfortunately, security is the type of job that can be stopped quickly by whoever hires the security firm. That is what happened here, and Donna was laid off. As was her pattern, when things got tough, she ended up working her prostitution gig again.

She did have a couple of romantic relationships during her five years in San Diego. She became engaged to one man, and they were pretty close for a time. Then she got close to another man, and there were others in the hopes of the romantic dream. She sent pictures of her boyfriend's home to her brother and mother, showing that she was happy and trying to live a good life.

While they broke up, Donna did find one more man with whom she fell in love. This was near the end of her time in San Diego, and he talked about the two of them finally moving back east. At that point, Donna felt she was ready. She had been through a great deal and had grown into a mature woman. That could have been the ending of her time in San Diego if her life was not cut short.

Donna wanted to return home, even to visit, but money was always the problem. She told her brother that she was saving up and as soon as she had her first week of vacation with the security job, she would come home to visit. She was laid off from that job before it could happen. Louis had the same money issues in trying to get out to California to see his sister. Finances were always a roadblock to either of them to make the cross-country journey.

There was always another roadblock in making it back home. Donna needed a truck and a trailer to bring her horse home with her. To support herself in an apartment, she took a job at an equestrian center as a trail guide. Since she and her brother Lou shared a love of horses, this was a sure sign of security and hope that one day life would change. You see, that love for horses always stayed with Donna. She purchased a beautiful jet black horse and named her Fantasia, stabling her where she worked at the "Little Red Riding" barn in Sorrento Valley, California, with her friend Michele Tennies. She bought her horse from Bill Collins at Equestrian Center in Ramona, where she also worked as a trail guide. In Donna's mind, if she was going to leave the area, her and Fantasia were a package deal that would be traveling together.

While Donna used contacts she made in prostitution and other walks of life to help her live a fairly stable life, her streetwalking gave her a support system early on in her new city. She hung around with other prostitutes. The girls tended to congregate at a 7-Eleven or laundromat in the area of El Cajon Boulevard. They were places they could use the bathroom, buy little things they needed, and feel safe. Some of Donna's early friends came from the girls who walked the street with her. For someone who craved friends who understood her after her days in Philadelphia, this was like hitting the jackpot.

There were girls like Donna who did prostitution out of a sense of desperation as she did. It was survival, not a life choice. There were good, likable girls like Donna, and these are probably the ones she gravitated to and struck up a real friendship with while in the city. She had to learn the customs and protocol of how to be a prostitute, and I am sure some girls helped her when she was getting started. Donna used her intelligence from there to figure things out.

It is easy to see that Donna made it work for herself and more. She did not use prostitution as an end game, but as a jumping off platform to try and advance herself. Donna did not have the luxury of training for a new life and then going after it. She had to make it up as she went and tried to figure everything out on the fly. Donna learned strength from her life experiences and somewhere in between the strength was the vulnerability and fear. We learn to be strong from what we encounter in life, and it can essentially teach you how to love yourself. Looking back at her five years there, she went from a girl with no skills when she arrived in San Diego, to a young woman who did more than survive; she began to thrive.

In the end, nobody could consider Donna a "typical" prostitute of the early 1980s in San Diego. She had a car, an apartment of her own, a horse, and she was well-spoken and dressed nicely. She had a nice book of clients and didn't hang out on the street anymore waiting for people to pick her up. She was on the cusp of leaving that life behind and trying to live the fairytale with a man she loved.

That ending never happened because there was another support group Donna used to help her quell the fear and insecurity of her life. This was the police in San Diego. The relationship between cops and prostitutes was confusing, to say the least. Cops had to arrest prostitutes on occasion but would also look out for them, at least the ones they liked or who would do favors for them. Cops would even be instrumental in keeping prostitutes out of jail.

This was a brand-new world that Donna found herself in. It would be a world that would greatly enhance her life in some ways. It would lead to contacts and more networking opportunities that would help her live in San Diego. Unfortunately, it also led to her death.

I still remember back in 1982 she sent Christmas cards to our home; and of course she loved her brother and would always look out for him, making sure that he followed the clean path in life, unlike her own at that moment. She was smart enough to know the difference. She would talk about her horse and how much she cared for Fantasia. At one time she expressed she was riding her horse without a saddle because his back was hurt. Aside from the path Donna was on she truly had an understanding of family values and love.

5

Prostitution - Police - Politics

Sex in exchange for something has been going on since men and women have been on the earth. It is always considered the world's oldest profession. In general, when we think of prostitution, we think of it as sex for money. While there are some women, and a few men, who make a very good living as a prostitute, they are the exception. Some finish servicing clients themselves and establish networks of other sex workers to make money off them. In the old days, these were the madams or owners of bordellos and whorehouses. Many of these owners tried to make their places safe for the girls to ply their trade. Other than a few locations in Nevada, these were illegal establishments. While still illegal, now the trend is to build that network on the internet.

For the most part, prostitution is not the haven of entrepreneurs but of people trying to survive. We will focus on the female side of prostitution here, and for a girl with limited skills and out on her own, prostitution was a way to survive.

For some, it was a temporary stop-gap measure that allowed them to live. These girls had their eye on other opportunities as they took money for sexual favors. Most are more than happy to take on a regular job when they have the chance. Other girls succumb to the lure of drugs, and prostitution ends up becoming the way to feed their habit. Instead of a temporary bridge of support, prostitution turns into a way of life and a never-ending whirlpool they can't leave.

Others used the money to help them learn a trade or career. Today, there are websites where girls in school are looking for "sugar daddies" who will help them pay for their education in return for the girl's company. This is a higher level of prostitution since the girls are only looking for one or a minimal number of backers who have the money to pay them. It is a means to an end, but the girl is going to have to deal with the fact one day that she used her body to get to be a lawyer, doctor, or CEO of a company. For some, it won't matter; for others, there might be psychological scars that will plague them the rest of their lives.

Back in the '80s, there was no internet. For a city like San Diego, the warm weather, ocean, and California life-style were a magnet to thousands of girls like Donna. That meant girls, many who were runaways like Donna, flocked to the area. When you have a glut of a certain demographic like young women with minimal education and marketable skills, it causes a labor problem. You have too many girls trying for jobs like waitresses, retail clerks, and whatever else was available back then. Inevitably, hunger and desperation steered a girl to prostitution.

Without any easy way of advertising, girls had to advertise themselves on the street. Dressing sexy and hanging out in a known area where men knew they could find whores was the basic business plan for a young prostitute. There were always areas in any major city where you could find the prostitutes hanging out. Depending on the police activity, the group might move away for a day or two to a different area, but they always tended to return to the accepted street or neighborhood. If you were a man and new to a city, you did not need to search too hard to find someone to tell you where the hookers were.

Prostitution corner

In San Diego, the place to find sex was El Cajon Boulevard. Now, prostitution was part of San Diego's history as far back as people can remember or history records. After World War II, the constant presence of the Navy and Marine Corps in San Diego certainly provided plenty of customers for the girls. El Cajon Boulevard was a natural place for the girls to hang out since a lot of traffic flowed through the area. It was also an area containing many adult entertainment businesses, so the prostitutes knew it was a haven for potential customers.

49 / Anita DeFrancesco

Even after the city forced those adult businesses to move away, El Cajon was still the "prostitute area," specifically near the area of 30th Street. The City of San Diego went through major periods of redevelopment like any other city. However, it never touched the hooker section of El Cajon. To show you how little that has changed, here is an excerpt of an article by Keegan Kyle in 2009:

Daybreak along El Cajon Boulevard can be a rude awakening and a reminder of the road's most illicit reputation.

A few women dressed in short skirts, leather jackets, and high heels waited this morning near the boulevard's intersection with Kansas Street. A motorist pulled up next to the group, one woman slid into the front passenger seat, and the car took off.

Across the street, customers at a 24-hour diner worked on their breakfasts and read the newspaper as if part of a normal routine. They turned to watch the remaining women when a patrolling black and white pulled up.

The police officers separated the remaining two women for questioning, but eventually let them walk away. They had no evidence to prove the women committed a crime, and at least for the time being, the women had lost their interest in standing at that corner. They'll be somewhere else tomorrow.

The corner of Kansas Street and El Cajon Boulevard is one block south of a YMCA youth activity center, less than one mile away from several schools and not too far from popular neighborhoods. It is also within a five-block radius where San Diego Police arrest the most people for crimes of prostitution. The boulevard is renowned as the city's hub of prostitution, and its reputation has helped sustain the level of criminal activity while other hotspots have faded with time.

From Donna's phone calls, this was not much different than the world she found herself in back in 1980. There were a lot more girls that walked the streets than now. They came in all sizes, shapes, races, and from different backgrounds. For a beginning prostitute, it was a matter of waiting for a car to pull over to you, see what you charged, and if there was agreement on price and services, the girl jumped in the car and off you went. Everything might happen in the car, or the guy took her someplace to have sex.

As you can imagine, this was never the safest way to make money. You didn't usually know who you were getting in the car with or what would end up happening. You were taking your life in your hands. If you worked for a pimp, you might have had the pimp's protection from the "Johns" looking for sex, but then you had to worry about how the pimp treated you. For someone like Donna who worked on her own and not for a pimp or anybody else, then you had to live by your wits and what you learned from hard-won experience on the streets.

On top of the personal danger, prostitution was illegal. Next to drugs, prostitution is one of the biggest underground economies in a city. The ironic part is that this illegal occupation would constantly be parading up and down a major thoroughfare such as El Cajon day and night. Being illegal and being right in the face of the rest of the city, this meant that besides the jerks she came into contact with, Donna also had to deal with the police.

In modern civilization, at least in America, prostitution was tolerated up until somewhere in the nineteenth century. By "tolerated," I mean there would be certain buildings or houses in towns where everyone knew the whores were, but nobody did anything about them. At the most, the police, or whatever the form of law enforcement existed for a town, would keep places from becoming too lewd or a disruption in town. It was not exactly a form of "don't ask, don't tell," but more of the ostrich approach: stick your head in the sand and pretend it isn't there.

This worked out until there was a push to expose prostitution for what it was and try to eradicate it. Obviously, this didn't happen, as you can find it now by checking local ads on the internet, but prostitution vs. police became a long-running conflict that continues today. The relationship between prostitutes and police is an interesting study. For one thing, prostitution has always been so widespread that it is impossible to corral. Second, it is rarely looked at in the same way as murder, robbery, assault, embezzlement, or drugs. While it is a point that people can heartily debate, prostitution is often rationalized as a victimless crime. The woman is exchanging services the man wants for money. Nobody is getting hurt, so it isn't always treated to the degree of other crimes.

Again, please realize that what I am stating here is the conventional rationalization of how the police department often looks at prostitution. With limited manpower, the police force in even a small city can't keep up with all the crime. The department must choose its priorities.

The truth is there are victims of prostitution. Most often, it is the prostitute. They can be physical victims of abuse, beatings, and even death. If Donna hadn't been a prostitute, she never would have been killed in 1985.

Many women who become hookers are already victims of their upbringing. Quite often abuse and problems in the family put women on the road to prostitution. On a sub-conscious level, women might choose prostitution to get back at the man that abused them because they can't seem to move on from the hate and scars of feeling used, abused, and having their innocence taken. Here, again, Donna is a classic example. Her uneven life growing up had to lead to an emotional upheaval for her regarding her relationship with men. Many women look at prostitution as a way to have some control over men since they often had men try to control them in the past or they look at it as a way to fill that empty void, that loneliness.

Police often took advantage of prostitutes by requesting bribes so that they wouldn't arrest the girls. This could be in the form of money or sexual favors. Both were acceptable payments for a cop to look the other way. A smart prostitute would take advantage of this system and zero in on one policeman or more so that she could keep doing her thing as hassle-free as possible. It was a cost to doing business, but if her cop friends kept her out of jail or warned her of an impending sweep of hookers in the neighborhood, then it was well worth it.

While prostitutes were not usually high on the crime list, they did have the problem of being disregarded as either victims or witnesses of a crime. Because of their profession, the prevailing thought if a girl witnessed a crime was, *"She's just a hooker. You can't take her word for anything."* If it were a case of her getting beat up or worse, a common expression would be, *"She was a prostitute. She probably had it coming."*

This is appalling, and I will talk about it more at the end of Donna's story. The important point to remember is that this was the prevailing thinking in most police department's in the 20th century, and certainly was the case in San Diego.

The San Diego Police Department's relationship with prostitutes was always sketchy. As I pointed out, prostitution was always prominent in places like El Cajon Boulevard. To maintain their public image, the police had to deal with the hookers. This entailed doing everything from picking up the occasional hooker to massive special task forces that swept the area where most of the prostitutes would be picked up. There would be an ebb and flow to the prostitution crackdowns.

There was a paradox to the legal penalties handed out to hookers when they were picked up. On the one hand, it was a crime, but the punishment wasn't too harsh. The first three times or so a prostitute was picked up, she would be subject to a night in jail, a fine, and doing some community service. After three such arrests, a prostitution crime would rise from a misdemeanor to a felony and the woman might have to do 90 days in jail. Prostitution was a very prevalent crime, but the penalties weren't all that bad.

Members of the San Diego Police often had connections or relationships with certain hookers. With so many on the street, they certainly had their choice. They would use the girls for sex if they could get away with it, but they also looked out for their favorites. A good example of this is when a cop would run the license plate of a potential new customer a girl was thinking of acquiring. This way the cop could make sure the guy wasn't a criminal and at least let the hooker know her new John seemed okay.

A smart woman used the police relationships to her advantage. If a hooker formed the right connections within the department, she could find breaks on rent, getting a car, shopping, and just about anything else she needed. Cops owned apartment houses and stores. They had plenty of contacts with whom they could hook up their favorite prostitutes. However, these relationships caused the department a lot of grief at times as they inevitably led to charges of corruption.

One of the problems with any police corruption is that it is hard to get a handle on it. You have to remember this was back in the '70s and '80s, when it seemed like every major city in America was battling police corruption. Cops were great at forming a "Blue Wall" when any of their brethren were under investigation, whether it was from Internal Affairs or an outside agency. It was a time before the news was 24/7 and newspapers did most of the news reporting. Unless a corruption incident was front-page news, there wasn't a great deal of interest about it from the public. When the public interest is nil, it is easy to sweep small corruptions under the rug.

One case in the early '80s not swept away was that of a Sergeant, a fifteen-year police veteran in the San Diego Police Department. In 1983, he was part of the department's Intelligence Division. In this role, the Sergeant, along with a former San Diego police officer, and a prostitute, were charged with running three prostitution businesses in the city. The police department threw that Sergeant off the police force. The Union newspaper reported that he was involved in the operation of a prostitution ring. The court sentenced all of them to jail.

This case showed how department administrators handled such situations when they came to the forefront. They took care of it quickly with minimal publicity. Though that Sergeant ultimately went to jail on an obstruction of justice charge, the prosecutor dropped the original charges of pimping and prostitution. The entire situation took six months to clear up with hardly a peep making it into the press. It was always the San Diego Police Department's goal to keep any negativity from the public.

Also in 2008, a 20-year veteran Detective assaulted an El Cajon prostitute and was let go. He had a history of pulling women over, searching them for drugs, and touching them inappropriately.

This is the backdrop of what prostitution was like in San Diego when Donna came on the scene. She was just another girl among many. However, she did stand out because she was pretty, carried herself well, was intelligent, and seemed to be of a different class than many of the streetwalkers.

While it was inevitable that she would come to the consideration of the police due to her profession, there were some on the force that would pay special attention to her. Donna quickly learned how to make those contacts work for her. It didn't always keep her from being picked up and charged for soliciting sex, but she did try to use those men to help make her life more comfortable. She also took advantage of anything they did that would help lead her out of prostitution towards a better life.

This is the stage Donna walked onto in San Diego. The time leading up to her death had her involved with individual cops. In a world where the lines were very gray between something illegal like prostitution and the cops who were supposed to stop it, it was not a cut-and-dried process figuring out what happened to her. Officially, Donna's death is still unsolved.

However, I have enough personal observations by some people involved at the time, news accounts, and a great deal of research to lay out the events and people involved with Donna leading up to when somebody killed her. I have my own opinions on the possibilities of who killed her and why, which I will share. However, if any reader sees anything in her story that might lead to a different conclusion than any of mine, please share. Ultimately, the only way to close the door on Donna's death with any sense of closure is through justice finally administered.

For the rest of Donna's story to make sense, it was important for you to understand San Diego in the 1980s and how prostitution and the police operated back in the day. It is an integral part of her few years living in the city, and probably what led to her death. As you will see, she became a pawn in a power struggle between two cops that ultimately led to her body discovered along the coast on that day in June.

6

Officer Larry Avrech

L arry Avrech began his career with the San Diego Police Department as a reserve officer in 1976. From November 1979 until January 1985, he worked as a regular academy policeman. He worked with Sgt. Norman Hardman in 1976, who passed away on August 18, 2016. Reserves went to the department's various station locations. They worked in patrols, providing all levels of law enforcement from the day-to-day duties of a patrol deputy to assisting in major emergencies. They also provided crowd and traffic control at community events and crime scenes. They had to complete police training and were on-call for so many hours a month. Reserve officers were either preparing for a career in law enforcement or were previous law enforcement personnel who still wanted to be involved.

In Larry's case, he was getting ready to join the police force. He was in the reserves for four years before becoming a full-time cop. Right from the beginning, Officer Avrech's relationship with the San Diego Police Department was rocky. One thing that is true about any police force is that they are a very close-knit group. It is certainly understandable when you are going out on the streets to "Protect and Serve." We see on the news what can happen to a cop on any patrol. It can be a dangerous job, especially in larger cities like San Diego. You are going to bond with your fellow officers and support each other.

Officer Larry Avrech.

Unfortunately, this bonding can go too far. It can also be a clique, and if a cop goes against the clique, he or she is going to be in for a difficult time. Cops are a very close group, and as I talked about in the last chapter, it can make getting an accurate story difficult for investigators because cops are great at circling the wagons. Right from the beginning, Larry Avrech was on the wrong side of the circled wagons.

When he became a permanent member of the San Diego Police Department in 1979, Larry alleges that the department was supposed to give him a raise. This was standard procedure for anyone making a move from the reserves to full-time cop. For whatever reason, whether it was a bureaucratic error or something else, Avrech didn't get his bump in salary. Instead of waiting to see if it would start after a few paychecks, Larry immediately made a motion about it. When you are a rookie on the police force, this is not the best way to make friends on the force. He felt that from that point on he was labeled a "troublemaker" and that there was a target on his back.

I understand why he did it. Most of us have had a job or two where we felt like our bosses treated us unfairly. You need to speak up. However, because Larry either lacked the patience or misunderstood the timeline for receiving his raise, he started off his career on the police department with a black mark in the eyes of other cops. In a close fraternity like the police, this is enough for your superiors and peers to ostracize you. Officer Avrech believed that the rest of the cops on the force didn't like him from that point on in his career. Police departments are a hotbed of gossip like anywhere else, and all it takes is a comment such as, "That guy is trouble," to be on the outside looking in.

How Avrech started his career with the cops is an important component of things that happened five years later when Donna died. Larry Avrech at times had a chip on his shoulder as it related to the other cops, and that comes through later in devastating ways for him, Donna, and others.

Larry Avrech became a cop right about the time Donna arrived in San Diego in 1980. It was 1981 when he and Donna had their first interaction. Since she was a prostitute and he was a cop, the usual conclusion is that they met when he picked her up for soliciting. That isn't what happened.

Larry alleges that he and Donna first ran into each other at a local 7-11 at Central and University Avenues in San Diego. Larry was on patrol and stopped there to pick up a magazine. He was in his uniform and overheard a cute older teenager telling the clerk, "I'd like to be a vice cop one day."

The teenager, of course, was Donna, and she just got out from her first overnight stay in jail after her initial arrest as a prostitute. Her first arrest came January 21, 1981. She had not been in the city too long, but she talked to enough girls in her business to know that becoming friends with the cops was something that would only help her. Donna was driving a Chevy and living in Menlo when she met Larry. I am not sure if she was innocently having that conversation with the clerk, but it was probably a case of seeing the uniformed police officer in the store and trying to get his attention. If that was her intent, it worked.

Larry was in his mid-twenties and didn't think it would be a bad idea to meet the attractive young woman, so he joined the conversation. He gave her some information of what it took to be a police officer. He told her that you could only move up to vice work in the department after you were in the division for a number of years.

Donna saying that she wanted to work vice was not simply a ploy to meet the young cop. Remember, this is a career she thought about, and she would soon be working for a security company as a step in that direction. She wanted to follow in the footprints of a family sheriff member whom she admired. I have no trouble believing that if life had worked out a little differently for Donna, she would have graduated high school and applied to be in a police department. Philadelphia had a huge force, and there were plenty of towns around the city and in New Jersey where she could have applied. So, she might have spoken up to get Avrech's attention in the store, but her interest was real.

Officer Avrech didn't know he was talking to a prostitute who had already been picked up once by his brother cops. He didn't patrol El Cajon Boulevard, and San Diego is a big city. Besides, Avrech alleged he had been off for the past two days, which is when the police arrested Donna. In the course of their conversation, he offered Donna a chance to participate in a "sponsored ride along."

Now, a police ride-along program allows community residents over 18 to accompany officers during their patrol in a police vehicle. If you had an interest in a police career, it was a good way to see what it was like on the job. It was also a good way to hang out with a pretty young girl who appeared needy and wanted to be a cop. Avrech wanted to impress Donna. He was no different than any other man; he was attracted to pretty women.

For Donna, it brought her close to a cop. She had her dreams and was interested in a law enforcement vocation, so the ride along helped fuel that desire. It probably also made her feel safe. While she flirted with Larry in the store, she was looking for security and anything that made her feel comforted. After all, prostitution wasn't a career choice, and I am sure her first overnight stay in jail shook her a little. She agreed to go on the ride along.

Officer Avrech reported to Sergeant Carver who was his immediate boss at the time but not the regular chief. He checked in with him for approval to take Donna on the ride along. Donna filled out a waiver for liability purposes and

handed it into the department. Later that day Avrech picked up Donna at her apartment.

During the ride along on March 19, 1981, Avrech alleges Donna saw a bit of what goes on in a cop's life. Avrech wrote tickets, stopped at certain locations to look around to see if everything was okay, and then took his break for dinner at the Taco King Mexican restaurant where he and Donna ate before going back on the ride along. This restaurant was one of the favorite places for cops to stop and eat in that part of San Diego.

While in the restaurant, Avrech alleged that his squad buddies started pulling up and noticed him and Donna eating. He said that they gave him some strange looks. They knew something that Avrech didn't. They recognized Donna as a prostitute arrested two days earlier. Who knows the cops' exact thoughts, but it had to seem strange to them that Avrech was with someone who had just been released from jail the day before. His "buddies" reported what they saw to Sergeant Carver.

When the shift was over, Avrech dropped Donna off at her apartment. He alleges that Donna began crying in the car and saying that she was lonely and had no friends. Avrech wanted to help Donna because he liked her. He claimed he was showing her compassion when she broke down, and he returned to her apartment when he got off duty. She was outside waiting, and she got in his car and they took off. A friendship between Donna and Avrech developed.

The two of them rode around. Avrech alleges they ended up parking somewhere and talking. I suspect that if Donna and Avrech had sexual encounters, then this perhaps was the beginning. Men love needy women, and having someone like Donna showing so much vulnerability was like winning the lottery. On her part, Donna wanted security, friends, and a daddy figure, and so men were the answer. Donna looked up to Larry as she would any male friend. She also knew that offering any sexual favors would help seal the friendship.

Donna realized the power sex had on men. However, she was still a lonely, scared child. She plunged into a new life that had its insecurities and dangers. It was surely a painful journey. Only a woman in her shoes could know the feelings she battled. Donna did feel safe around her policemen friends. She mingled and dabbled with a few of them after Avrech. She looked to them for support and empathy.

Avrech said that Donna was a smart girl who had a charm whereby she could get what she wanted because people liked her. A girl in her position needed to survive, and her quality of niceness made people like her, and so they provided help. Any girl in her position would learn tactics to save and protect herself and make herself better, no matter what it took. No woman wants to work on the streets all her life. Officer Larry Avrech was one of the first of her police friends, but he wouldn't be the last.

Larry thought he met a nice, vulnerable girl that he thought might be good to spend some time with or even more. However, trouble started for Avrech the next day. Information from the other cops at the Taco King got back to Sergeant Carver, who filled out a report. Carver was not the regular chief for Avrech's unit. If the regular guy had been on, he might have known about Donna being recently picked up and nixed the entire ride along. He could have filled Avrech in on who Donna was.

Such are the little things that affect lives. If the regular sergeant were on duty, perhaps the events never would have unfolded the way they did over the next five years. What happened instead was that Officer Avrech's trials and tribulations with the department that started badly when he made noise about getting his raise became worse. When Larry went back to the station after the ride along, he had to fill out papers. Other cops started teasing him that he was doing things incorrectly and that he was filling out the paperwork wrong. They said you must be hiding stuff. He still did not realize that Donna was a hooker. As it turned out, he did forget to ask her to fill out an evaluation form regarding the ride along.

The day after the ride along, Avrech alleges he took off from work because of a back injury that was bad enough for him to go to the hospital. When he returned to his home, Sergeant Ed Sammons, an investigator, called Avrech and told him that he needed to come down to the station because they needed to talk. Avrech couldn't figure out what this was all about and he became very confused and apprehensive.

He quickly found out. The department was starting an investigation concerning the ride along with Donna. The question they posed to him was, "Did you go on a 'date' with Donna Gentile?" "Date" in this context meant did Larry have a sex date with a prostitute, not a date in the normal vernacular. He told them that it wasn't like that and it was simply a ride along and the dinner. Larry alleged they circled and started putting the pressure on him. They asked him all kinds of questions that did not pertain to the investigation, such as what kind of cars he drove. When he told them that he had a Datsun F10 and a Chevy Caprice, they proceeded to insinuate that it takes a lot of gas to keep those cars going and that he must be rich. That meant he must have money to pay prostitutes. They continued to badger Avrech in this way.

When Sergeant Sammons told Avrech that the department was investigating a complaint that Avrech had been with a prostitute, Larry became angry. Getting mad wasn't good for his image since he had already been labeled a malcontent by the "where is my raise" fiasco when he first got on the force. That was a class action suit that Larry orchestrated for himself and others. Sammons pressured Avrech more. He was looking for a confession and wanted an answer if Larry had sex with Donna, a known prostitute. Avrech never admitted to having sex with Donna. With only a year on the new job, this made it worse for him for the rest of the time on the force. It wasn't a good start.

Avrech alleges he stayed out on sick leave for six weeks with the back injury. The department didn't leave him alone at home. Sergeant Art Truman came over with a smooth story to try and hook Avrech into a web. He told Larry that the department wanted the truth because if he had sex with a prostitute and he got a disease from her, they needed to know that. The department manipulated him in this way with the hopes to get him to come clean, even though if he said he had sex with Donna, the department would fire him. They even questioned Donna. Neither of them ever admitted to sex taking place, and the department had to give up on their efforts to get a confession.

However, when Avrech returned to work after recovering from the injury, the department placed

a warning in his file with regards to the ride along because he failed to follow the established procedure. Lt. Howell and Lt. Roulette Armstead signed it on April 19, 1981:

Employee: Officer Larry Avrech # 2900
  (WARNING LETTER)
Date: April 19, 1981
Department/Division: Police Eastern Patrol

On March 19, 1981, Officer Larry Avrech took Donna Gentile on a ride-a-along and failed to follow the established procedure for ride-a-longs as set forth in the Police Department Instructions. Officer Avrech violated Rule XI, Section 3 (d) of the Rules of the Civil Service Commission. (That the employee has violated any lawful or official regulation). To wit: Department Instruction 6.31 (Ride-a-longs). Section 5 (b) (Placing the appropriate comments on the back of the waiver form). Officer Avrech has been advised that further violations of this nature will result in more serious disciplinary action.

Signed,
Lt. Roulette Armstead
Lt. Howell

Rule XI, Section 3 (d) It reads: *That the employee has violated any lawful or official regulation or order or failed to obey any lawful*

*and reasonable direction given by a superior officer when such vio-
lation or failure to obey amounts to insubordination or serious breach
of discipline.* As it related to Avrech in this case, it means that
Donna didn't put her evaluation comments in about what
she learned and observed on the ride along. Perhaps Avrech
should have been more attentive in reviewing the form
before he handed it in. I believe this was a strike against him
since he wasn't one of the favorites, but policy is policy, and
the department looked for any reason to bring Avrech down.

Officer Larry Avrech Warning April 19, 1981.

If there was ever another incident against him, the
department could fire Avrech. They had him work in dis-
patch for a week before he was allowed back on patrol. While
stationed at the radio, Avrech alleges that some of the other
cops would tease and bully him about Donna and make
remarks such as "we arrested your girlfriend" and gave her a
"choke out." A choke out is done by a policeman if a criminal
becomes combative; it is a hand to hand combat tactic

involving the use of a chokehold to cause a temporary loss of consciousness, which is then released. Avrech explained that streetwalkers liked to intentionally get combative and fight with a police officer while resisting arrest because a "choke out" gave them a certain blissful sensation not to be confused with erotic asphyxiation.

Because he had the warning in his file, Avrech wasn't able to move up in the San Diego Police Department in the way that he expected. He was passed over for any promotions during his tenure on the force. With the Donna incident, the target he already had on his back in regards to the police department became bigger. He was definitely on their "shit" list, and the chip on his shoulder only became bigger. From all other indications, Officer Larry Avrech was a good cop and was liked by some but not by all. He shared the many accolades in his file from citizens who wrote in saying he had caught a criminal or had helped them out in some way. Unfortunately, once you are on the bad side of the police force, especially if you are part of the force, it is difficult to get back into the good graces of the rest of the cops.

When Avrech returned to patrol duty, he patrolled north of the freeway while El Cajon Boulevard was south. There was no way for him to run into Donna when he was on duty. He certainly didn't have her in his squad car anymore after that incident.

It is difficult to know how close Donna and Larry were after their first encounter. I would speculate that just as when any two people first meet, and there is some attraction, they might have hung around with each other quite a bit in the beginning. It probably faded quickly as Larry had to keep his police career going with little support from his superiors and Donna was going back and forth between prostitution, getting into security work, horses, and involvement with other men. I am sure that Donna and Larry ran into each other off and on over the next four years or so before they became intertwined again. They shared a friendship that turned combatant towards the end.

As you will see, a chance encounter at the 7-Eleven and becoming something of friends would explode five years down the road. In hindsight, the ride along became the catalyst for Donna's death. Because of that, Officer Larry Avrech became more of a pariah and an outcast in the department. As you will see, this drove him to orchestrate a few events that would be bad for him and others, while being catastrophic for Donna.

There are a few more players and incidents that come into Donna's life that propels this tragedy forward. The next four years doesn't have much of Larry Avrech in them other than as a friend and acquaintance of Donna's. Again, this entire story hinges on how a chance meeting or event can turn a person's life around. I believe that if anything I related so far or in the next chapter didn't occur, Donna's story would have been so different.

7

Donna, Lieutenant Black and Internal Affairs

Avrech wasn't the only cop in Donna's life. She was a smart girl, and she knew it wouldn't hurt her to have some cops on her side. It would mean sexual favors for some, but Donna looked at it as a way to make her life a little easier. Other prostitutes took advantage of the quid pro quo with members of the San Diego Police Department when they could.

You have to remember that with the corruption in the San Diego Police Department at that time in the 1980s, it wasn't like the cops were new to this. The truth is that the cops had the luxury to be very selective with the girls they chose. For them, El Cajon Boulevard was like a buffet of women for them. Prostitutes came in all varieties of looks, races, skills, and backgrounds. Just as a man looking for a hooker had a certain type, the cops did too.

Here, Donna had a decided advantage. She was attractive, bright, neat, and basically, a sweet girl. She had class and cops picked her out as a special case. Donna was a girl you could take home to your mother. She lived in San Diego, so she wasn't a transient. Drugs and alcohol were not Donna's thing. She may have tried them, but it was something that wasn't for her. Her only passion was her horse Fantasia. Donna would lecture and play mother to her brother from afar and tell him in letters not to drink. She always reprimanded him on the telephone.

It was an arrangement that worked for Donna when she was working the streets. It didn't seem like she kept in contact with the cops much when she wasn't hooking. For somebody as young as Donna, she was very pragmatic about her life. She certainly embodied the word "survivor." Donna had an instinct to do what she needed to do so that she could keep a roof over her head and food on the table. Don't forget; this was a 17-year-old who went across the country as a runaway and decided to stay and make a go of it. What she didn't know, she learned from others. With everything else, she made it up as she went.

A hallmark of Donna's short five years in San Diego is that she moved around a great deal, sharing rooms or apartments with other girls or men with whom she got involved. Donna was a slave to her finances like anybody else trying to make ends meet, and she swung between steady jobs like the security company and prostitution. When Donna worked security, she did take up with the man who was much older than her, but she didn't want to have sex with him and moved on after a bit.

Donna was like any other young woman. She wanted to fall in love with a man and live happily ever after. She did have a couple of real love relationships while she was in San Diego. One was with a man named Pete who was five years older than her. They started living together in 1983 and rented an apartment. They were a solid couple and even owned a Buick together. This was the steadiest relationship Donna had ever had up to that time. Unfortunately, it was not meant to last. She repeatedly lived the roller-coaster lifestyle but knew what stability was and longed for that. She told her brother that she and Pete were not getting along, and soon she was back on her own. She went to great lengths to keep herself connected to her family.

The only other real relationship I know of that Donna was in was a man she was seeing at the time of her death. I know they were talking about moving away from California and coming back east, but, sadly, she never had a chance to return or see where life would have taken her with that young man.

As you can see, the life of a young runaway who was in and out of prostitution was ungrounded and unsettled. Donna was a restless soul who wanted to settle down or at least have some stability and build roots. In her world, one of the consistent contacts she had was with the cops.

Some she met because they patrolled the area where she worked. Others, like Larry Avrech, she happened to meet and took them wherever it went. Even cops she hadn't met yet might have known of her. This was either because of her record and reputation as a prostitute or through other cops who knew her.

As I mentioned earlier, police departments are very close. It can work in a cop's favor, depending on what side of the blue wall you were on. If you were like Larry Avrech and ticked people off right from the start, you were going to be kept on the outside looking in. Cops like that didn't advance through the department. Their fellow officers shunned them, and they didn't fare too well with their supervisors.

However, if you were part of the "in" crowd within the department, you had friends all over and a certain amount of respect. People had your back, they invited you to social outings, and people accepted you. You shared information with your fellow cops covering a whole host of things that were going on in the department and the city. You even shared girls.

I don't mean this regarding a cop orgy where they passed girls around, but if a cop had a working girl for a friend, that girl was considered a cut above the other prostitutes. While she wasn't an untouchable when raids or vice details tried to clean up the streets, she was given more breaks by cops when possible.

This is where Donna found her sweet spot for a time in San Diego. She had a network of cops who looked out for her in various ways. I was told that the last apartment building she occupied in La Mesa was owned by a sheriff and corporation partners. When someone would come into her place, one of the first things the person would see would be the police department emblem on the wall. Maybe Donna wasn't quite branded as one of their own, but it was close!

I don't know everything in her life that was provided by cops, but she did okay. She even went to a feed store owned by a cop to buy food for her beloved horse. Being that owning and caring for a horse isn't cheap, this gives you some insight into how Donna could own one. Cops liked her, and she took advantage of it. I am sure she didn't do a lot of this only to see how much she could get out of the cops. For her, the police were a source of security for her. After all, her job could be dangerous. Plus, she did have aspirations to get into law enforcement eventually. In addition to leaving the world of prostitution, that is a big reason she leaped at the security job when she had the opportunity.

One cop that would play a big part in her life was Lieutenant Carl Black. Lt. Black had a soft spot for Donna. He genuinely liked her and felt compassion for the young woman. I do not have any intimate details on their relationship, but the general picture of them together is enlightening.

Lt. Carl Black

Lt. Black allegedly came from money, and he wanted to help Donna. For a time, he was the head of the prostitution detail, which is probably how he learned about her. I am not sure exactly when they met, but it was somewhere around 1984. Donna was a charmer and, at first, she probably realized that a cop with Black's rank dealing with the prostitutes in San Diego would be a great contact to have. He certainly had the power to pull some strings in her favor if an occasion warranted it.

According to Avrech's perception of Lt. Black, he was a calculating man. Larry alleged that when Black first came on board to the eastern division in the department, his greeting was cold and callous. It went something like this, "Hello, the door is open. I don't like liars, or you get fired." That was the extent of his greeting. Black demanded honesty, and when Avrech heard of his dealings with prostitutes he labeled Black as a hypocrite. There were rumors that Black had trouble with other women. The department often praised Black, which raised him up in the eyes of other cops.

As Black and Donna got to know each other, a genuine friendship developed between the two of them. For Donna, he was a strong father figure for her. This was definitely lacking in her life for a long time. It is no stretch of the imagination to see a girl whose dad died when she was young and then had to deal with the other challenges she was later faced within her homelife to have a void inside of her that such a man as Lt. Black could fill it.

Colorado River Basin

Black liked Donna. He saw a great deal of potential in her and wanted to rehabilitate her. He knew she didn't want to be a prostitute and that she had a great deal of potential for a better life. I am sure that sex was part of the friendship between the two of them, but it sounded like there were a real connection and affection here. Lt. Black could have been the ultimate sugar daddy for Donna, not only regarding how he might have helped her financially and within the department, but as a real shot for her to focus on a career path that would have taken her out of the sex trade for good.

One place that the friendship took them was when Carl Black took Donna with him on the annual Colorado River trip. Now, the Colorado River is a major river of the western United States that starts in the Rocky Mountains in Colorado. It flows southwest through the Colorado Plateau country of western Colorado, southeastern Utah and northwestern Arizona, where it cuts through the Grand Canyon. It turns south near Las Vegas, Nevada, goes into Lake Mead and then along the Arizona–California border before entering Mexico. They camped out at Martinez Lake in Martinez, Arizona, along the Colorado River. It was 35 miles from Yuma County.

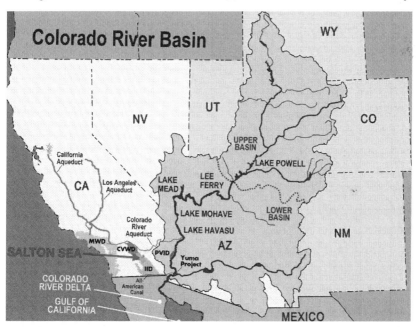

The Colorado River vacation trip was a weekend initiated by Lieutenant Carl Black and a girlfriend, plus two other couples. Jeff Fellows was with a girlfriend, and Sergeant Kevin Hargrove was the date set up for Donna that weekend. When questions arose in the later investigation, Hargrove said he had no idea that Donna was a prostitute.

Larry Avrech alleged that the Colorado River excursions were regular trips where cops would take prostitutes for a getaway, and the cops would receive sexual favors in exchange for lighter sentences or other breaks. As we will see in the next chapter, Avrech comes into play with this outing in a big way, and this trip was one of the key points that figured prominently in Donna's last months.

Donna was in a position where she needed help. It was at around this time that she was picked up for the third time for soliciting sex. It was her third strike, and that meant more than an overnight stay in jail. She had to go to prison for three months. On April 28, 1984, Donna was living on Spring Street in La Mesa. Lt. Black intervened on her behalf and made a call to her probation officer. Black told the officer that she wasn't the run-of-the-mill transient prostitute. She had a lot going for her, and Black said that she could make a break from prostitution. Lt. Black impressed the officer and, in the end, Donna went to jail on a work furlough program. Work furlough inmates showed maturity and stability both in the prison facility and community. This meant that she left jail in the morning to look for a job and had to return by a certain time in the late afternoon. It was about as good as jail can get.

Black did a lot for her beyond this. He made many other calls on her behalf. Carl Black even paid for a $1,000 of Donna's legal fees. Keep in mind that $1,000 was pretty big money 35 years ago, and it paid for a lot more of a lawyer's time than it does now. It was a significant amount for a cop to put out for a prostitute, especially a cop of high rank within the San Diego Police Department.

I will be coming back to Lt. Black in the next chapter as all the players are coming together in this tragedy. We have Donna, Officer Avrech, and Lt. Black. One young girl and two cops make up the main players of this drama, but there is one more periphery player. That player consisted of other cops.

These cops are from Internal Affairs. They are the ones that investigate other cops for wrongdoing. If you were a child, Internal Affair cops were the kids nobody liked because they told on everyone else. Nobody likes a snitch, and there is natural resentment towards the department that other cops felt were always looking over their shoulder. I doubt there was a lot of social interaction between most of the police department with Internal Affairs investigators.

Donna figures into this group because IA recruited her to be an informant. When jail looked like a real possibility for Donna, she panicked as almost anyone would facing prison. While she knew cops like Black, Avrech, and others, she didn't know if they could keep her out of jail. She wanted to exercise all options at her disposal to avoid going there. The facts are sketchy if she offered her services to Internal Affairs or if they sought her out, but she became an informant.

Since it was IA, they were interested in dirty cops, so that is where they sent Donna. For Donna to fulfill her duties as a police informant for the Internal Affairs Department of the San Diego Police Department, she had to snitch on the police. This placed her in the middle of multiple police sting operations and one big scandal. She often had to wear a wire where Internal Affairs recorded her conversations with any cops. She would also be expected to help on reports compiled on suspected dirty policemen.

Her IA work put Donna in dangerous positions as she found herself in the middle of drug or prostitution stings. In general, she would be there to observe if a cop took a bribe, whether it be money, drugs, or sexual favors to look the other way or let somebody go. That is a generalization, but you get the idea. She was working with the police to catch other cops who were corrupt. There is an irony here since some of her best friends on the police force were corrupt in their own way during their dealings with Donna.

It doesn't matter if you are in the mob, corporate America, or a police department; nobody likes a snitch. This is especially true when the people you are informing on have a feeling of entitlement and power. To them, it becomes almost second nature to treat a suspected snitch with contempt and violence. Nothing is more dangerous than a powerful person about to be brought down from his or her perch.

Donna was gambling that the danger was worth the opportunity to avoid jail time. As you know, she didn't get out of it, though Black's efforts made jail as painless as possible. In the grand scheme of what happened, I am sure Donna would have traded in those 90 days in jail for being able to live a long life.

In the next chapter, we will explore how everyone we talked about in the past two chapters comes together. There was a real triangle between Donna, Avrech, and Black. It is not a love triangle, but one of power and perceived slights. As for Internal Affairs, involving Donna with their work could also have led to her demise. What it all comes down to is a tragic end to a lovely young woman whose associations with the cops presumably had a lot to do with her death.

8

The Triangle

Donna Gentile came into contact with Officer Larry Avrech again sometime in June of 1984. They had run into each other off and on since their initial encounter a couple of years earlier. Avrech continued working as a patrolman. Donna alleged that he initiated the contact when he asked her to have sex with him during a vice unit crackdown on prostitution. Lieutenant Carl Black was in charge of the detail, and Donna alleged that Avrech would give her a break if she had sex with him. Donna didn't see any way out of it and gave into Avrech. Donna alleged that she and Larry had sex a handful of times during the summer and that she looked to Officer Avrech for protection.

Sometime after the Colorado River excursion, Donna ran into Officer Larry Avrech again in a laundromat. It was one of the places the prostitutes liked to hang out. When Avrech saw her on this particular day, Donna had a bandage on her foot from when she hurt it on the trip. He asked Donna how she injured the foot, and she told him a little about the Colorado River weekend. Donna told Avrech that Black took her to the Yuma Medical Center; she used an alias and he paid for the medical care of her foot. Avrech says that the lieutenant (Black) who demanded honesty of his fellow cops took a known prostitute to the Colorado River, procured her for a sergeant friend, and allowed her to give false information at a medical facility. This set Avrech over the top.

Carl Black   Donna Gentile   Larry Avrech

Avrech was still smarting from the warning that had been placed in his file when he first took Donna on the ride along. It had been an obstacle for him to receive any consideration for promotion. He felt that he went to school to be a cop and when he looked around at the other men in the department, he saw people that he considered inferior to himself moving up. He had friends on the police force, but he wasn't exactly the most popular cop around. Even with letters in his file from citizens he had helped during his duties, he was still a patrolman with no real future in the department that he could see.

When Larry Avrech got wind that Lt. Carl Back had been out on a trip with a known prostitute, he had the beginnings of an idea. Black was one of his superiors, and it frustrated Avrech that the lieutenant was having an affair with Donna while the police department severely penalized him for driving her around one night in an approved community service function.

For Avrech, it became a point of what was good for the goose was good for the gander. From his viewpoint, Avrech saw this as a golden opportunity to take down Black and to make things right. Larry discovered that Black had bailed Donna out of jail after one of her arrests and had been paying her medical and legal expenses. Avrech thought this was something Internal Affairs should know about Lt. Carl Black.

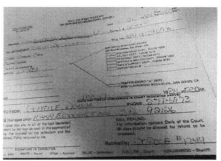

Bail receipt.

In Avrech's mind, it came down to simple revenge. Even though Black didn't have anything to do with the warning that went into Larry's file, the lieutenant became a symbol of everything wrong with the San Diego Police Department. Black had rank and seemed to do whatever he pleased. He was also well-respected and well-liked in the department, which was everything Avrech wasn't. Though Black had more contacts in Internal Affairs than Avrech did, Larry still launched his campaign to bring Black down.

The first thing he believed he needed from Donna was more information, and, hopefully, proof from her. Even though they were acquaintances and even friends, Larry started to harass Donna. She said she had photographs from the Colorado River trip that Black was getting developed for her and Avrech started to press her for them. If he could take pictures to Internal Affairs that lieutenants and sergeants of the department were cavorting with known prostitutes on a fun weekend trip, it would force IA to act on the information.

Then, if the investigators decided to dig in further, Avrech figured that they would find evidence of favors Black did for Donna.

By this time, Donna was a pro in manipulation. She had been living on her own in San Diego for almost five years and had a keen mind based on her years of manipulating men, whether they were customers, friends, or cops. There was no way she was going to give Black up to Avrech. There was a little something between her and Black that went beyond the usual relationship Donna had with a policeman. Donna wasn't only using him for her own gain. She liked him, and there was affection between them. Black did a great deal for her, and Donna wasn't a cold-hearted witch who took that for granted. She had always been looking to get out of the prostitute racket, and she knew that Black was genuinely helping her to find a way to do so.

For Donna, running into Avrech at this time was advantageous for her. Between February and March of 1984, she was charged with prostitution three more times. Because of this, she was soon to face sentencing to at least three months of jail time. She had Black batting for her and her work as an informant for Internal Affairs as possible leverage to keep her from going to jail. Black didn't know yet if he could arrange something like the work furlough program that Donna eventually would take part in during her prison sentence. To Donna, if she could secure more positive influences when she went before the judge and asked for leniency, then all the better for her.

Now you had Avrech who saw a way to get back at some of the higher-ups in the police department for all the perceived slights he received since joining the force. Then there was Donna, who was trying to find more brownie points to try and stay out of jail. You certainly had two people cut from the same cloth. They were both looking for different angles to get what they wanted. Donna and Larry could have made a nice team had they been in cahoots together. In this case, though, they were both trying to play each other. When you had two intelligent people doing this, it became a game of chess to see who would win. Larry and Donna may have been at war with each other, but in the end, the common thread they shared was they both battled the law and lost.

You see, Donna gave Larry the impression she would fork over the photographs of the Colorado River trip if he wrote a letter on her behalf to the judge to help with her sentencing. A letter coming from a cop carried a great deal of weight when it came down to the sentencing of an individual. Donna did whatever she could to convince Larry to do this for her. He eventually gave in and wrote her a letter to be used in her favor. Unfortunately, nothing is as simple as it should be and Officer Avrech wrote it on the wrong kind of paper. He originally composed the note on a piece of cardboard or the back of a ticket, something like that. You can't submit a letter from a cop written out in such a manner into a court case!

When Larry gave her the original letter, he also gave her fifty dollars, and they allegedly had sex while he was still in uniform. That type of transaction was a normal way of doing business for Donna, but she became angry when she saw how Larry wrote the letter. To her, it was just a careless and stupid thing to do. She went and brought him the proper paper to rewrite the letter, and he did do that for her. Here you see character reference letters Avrech wrote on Donna's behalf for her case. The letter written on the correct paper was without a complete date, which Larry knew was not permissible in a court. He was just smarting to gain those photographs.

Avrech's original letter for Donna on the wrong paper:

On 7-8-84, I was requested by Donna Gentile to be a character reference for her probation hearing. On 7-10-84 I contacted Probation Officer Burgenbach. She advised me that she was amazed that Donna would only be getting 45 days with all the priors that she had. She further stated that with good time off it would be reduced to 30 days. I first met Donna three years ago on an authorized police ride along. In dealing with her, she has always cooperated with the police. She does not have a history of using drugs. I feel that probation would be most beneficial than incarceration. I understand that at this time Donna Gentile is presently employed as a Security Guard and has not been working the streets.

Larry Avrech

Avrech's letter for Donna on the correct paper:

On 7/1984, I was requested by Donna Gentile to be a character reference for her probation hearing. On 7/84 I contacted Probation Officer Bergenbach. She advised me that she was amazed that Gentile would only be getting 45 days with all the priors she had. She further stated that with good time off the number of days would be reduced to 30. I advised her that I felt that this was highly irregular of a police officer to act as a character reference. In a case like this Burgenbach understood.

I advised Burgenbach that I had dealt with Donna Gentile in the past and had known her about 3 years. I further explained that I felt that Gentile was "atypical" of the prostitutes on the boulevard and that there were other girls more deserving of her fate. Burgenbach thanked me for calling and stated that she appreciated my calling. Burgenbach also told me that the sentence must be carried out by the judge whether he wants to or not and that regardless of what anybody did or said "she is going to do the jail time." This ended the discussion.

Larry Avrech

All of these things such as letters and phone calls always helped a case and sometimes resulted in less jail time or no jail at all. Again, Donna was an audacious person who didn't back down and was fighting for her life and rights. She believed in herself and was saving herself in any way possible.

Now that Larry did his part, he expected Donna to keep her end of the bargain, namely to give her photographic proof of the trip on the Colorado River. He had almost a bloodlust in his heart for turning Lt. Black into Internal Affairs for misconduct.

There were many mistakes made by both Donna and Larry in this whole affair. Perhaps the biggest one was on Avrech's part when he did not simply go to Internal Affairs when he first heard about Carl Black's apparent inappropriate interaction with a prostitute. Granted, there would be great hypocrisy there because Avrech was allegedly having sex with Donna at this time too. Nevertheless, if he went to IA, they would have to follow up on his complaint. Instead, Avrech was intent on conducting his investigation. It could have been because he either didn't trust Internal Affairs or he wanted to hand over everything about Black on a silver platter to ensure that they would act on it. Doing it on his own, though, ultimately backfired. In the end, Avrech brought down Donna and Black.

Donna, for her part, had the letter she wanted from Officer Avrech. It is hard to tell if she promised Larry the pictures from the Colorado River weekend. It could have been her way of teasing him by saying things like, "I have these things. I bet you could use them." I am not even sure if she showed them to Avrech, or if they existed at all. I also have to imagine if she were giving sexual favors to Avrech, she would have thought that was more than enough compensation for the letter he wrote.

Avrech didn't think so. He started pressing Donna for those photographs. He pushed her hard and allegedly started harassing Donna at every chance. There was no way Donna was going to do anything to get Black in trouble. This was the policeman helping her with her legal fees, trying to help her with the jail time, and even bailing her out when it was necessary. He had good contacts in the police department that he shared with Donna. Remember, even one of her apartments and horse feed were because of cops. You don't kill the goose that lays the golden egg when the goose is providing so much.

In some ways, Donna was also stringing Avrech along for her gain in addition to the endorsement letter she now had on her behalf. One of the mistakes Donna made at this time that would have further consequences on how everything unfolded is that she was still a prostitute. She was still actively making money at her trade. One of the things she relied on Avrech for was to alert her when vice raids were happening.

The San Diego Police Department did periodic crackdowns on prostitution in the streets. The two main methods were to catch a prostitute soliciting someone for sex or to harass the hell out of them until they moved away from El Cajon or wherever they were congregating. The harassment approach was to assign a bunch of uniformed cops to wherever the prostitutes were located. For example, the cops would follow the hookers around on El Cajon Boulevard and issue tickets for everything from dropping a cigarette butt on the sidewalk to jaywalking. This constant citing of minor offenses exasperated the prostitutes until they moved away. It didn't matter that they would be back soon enough. The point was that the people of San Diego would see the police doing their job and the department could trumpet its success.

As for taking a prostitute in for soliciting sex, this led

to one of Donna's arrests. At the arraignment for this particular charge, an Officer Rosenbloom testified to the events
that led to Donna's arrest. It was an undercover sting operation in which Rosenbloom alleges he made eye contact
with Donna. She came over to him without any invitation,
and they got in his car and drove around. Once they were
in the car, Donna solicited him for sex. After Rosenbloom
rejected this request, he delivered Donna to the vice unit on
El Cajon, and they arrested her. Here is Rosenbloom's arrest
report:

> *San Diego Police Department Investigators Report*
> *3-24-84*
> *Location: Rolando and El Cajun Blvd.*
> *Subject: Gentile*

> ### *OFFICERS STATEMENT*
> *On the above date and time, I was temporarily assigned to the
> vice unit as an undercover operator. I was dressed in casual clothes
> and driving an unmarked police vehicle. I have worked in this capacity
> on prior occasions and had been trained by other vice officers in the
> terminology and practice of prostitutes. I have made five arrests in
> this capacity and have assisted in arrests and transports of prostitutes
> on many numerous occasions.*
>
> *On 3-24-84 I was briefed again on the practices and terminology
> of prostitutes and their customers, commonly called johns and tricks.
> I was assigned to work the El Cajon Boulevard area.*
>
> *I was driving east on El Cajon Boulevard. I saw two girls on the
> southwest corner of Aragon and El Cajon Boulevard. I drove by two
> blocks advised my cover units by radio of my location and made a
> U-turn. I drove one block west of Aragon going west on El Cajon Bou-
> levard. I made another U-turn and stopped at Aragon and El Cajon.
> GENTILE came over to the passenger door and got into my car. The
> following conversation then took place.*

O-Officer   S-Suspect

S-What do you want to do?

O- I don't care I just want to have some fun.

S- Do you want some head? (common street term meaning oral copulation)

O- Yeah, that sounds good.

S- How much do you want to spend?

O- You tell me.

S- (Holding up four fingers) How about forty?

O- Hell, that's more than I expected. (Suspect held up one finger) I don't know, they're too many cars around here and it isn't worth the risk. Let's forget it.

I then let the suspect out of the car at Rolando and El Cajon. I then advised my cover officers by radio to arrest GENTILE. The officers made contact with GENTILE at Aragon and El Cajon and placed her under arrest for 647 (b) P.C. (Soliciting Prostitution) She was then transported to Las Colinas.

OFFICER A. ROSENBLOOM I.D. # 9945 Division: VICE

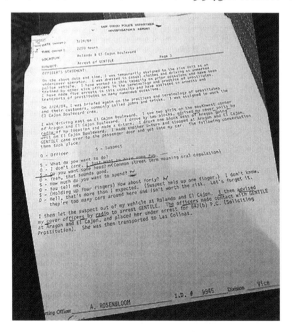

Here you see a conversation between an officer and a suspect. Officers are wired, and it is required they get the conversation on tape before they make the arrest. However, the risk for a prostitute is to talk about money and sex. That is why in this conversation Donna puts up the dollar amount in fingers, but then she lets her guard down as so many do because they begin to trust the enemy and end up saying, "How about forty?"

Talking about sex is one thing, but for an arrest to be made it has to be supported with the suspect asking for money and supporting it by saying they will use a condom. Because most prostitutes will use slang terms such as "head" or "full service," the vice officer needs to get the suspect to say sex and money or condom in the same conversation. Then they can make the arrest. The arrest is made based on the conversation and not during the act. In fact, the act should not happen.

On occasion, the cops have sex with prostitutes and then arrest them. Also, a clear sign that he is a cop is that he resists and acts like it's too much money instead of negotiating, or he becomes an unrealistic big spender to entice the prostitute. Prostitutes learn to look out for these types of conversations. One thing a lawyer will advise is never to talk about sex and money, and never solicit oneself. Sex workers have learned over the decades how to talk and how to solicit without getting criminalized. It is by far one of the most challenging aspects of the sex worker business. Today, especially in California, a female officer needs to be present in the wings after an arrest to protect the victim from the male cop. The female cop will make sure that the male cop doesn't touch her.

When Donna gave her testimony, she said that she went over to him and asked, "Don't I know you from three years ago?" She went on to explain that she recognized the officer as someone who offered to date her three years earlier. In prostitute parlance, "date" meant sex for money. Whether this was true or not, Donna gave the impression that it wasn't unusual to have a cop as a customer, which backs up the corruption issue concerning cops and prostitutes the San Diego Police Department was struggling with in the 1980s.

Having been the target of both harassment practices and a sting operation, any warnings that Avrech could give Donna that a crackdown unit was on the prowl would be a huge help. It was unfortunate for Donna that in a short period the police picked her up several times for prostitution. If she had a regular job of some sort at this point, she would have avoided so much of the trouble. Sadly, that didn't happen, and she was looking for ways to keep herself out of jail.

While waiting for the sentencing hearing, Larry Avrech allegedly kept the pressure on Donna to fork over the photos and Donna continued to string him along or refused him completely. Perhaps out of a feeling of desperation, Avrech started to become a real bother to Donna. The pressure became cumbersome for Donna up to this point along with everything else. You have to remember we are talking about a 22-year-old girl who had been living on the edge and by her wits for almost five years at this point. A person can only take so much stress. It was a psychologically and emotionally stressful time both for Donna and Avrech.

The chess game between Donna and Avrech now became a race. One of them needed to get their respective complaint to the police first. For Donna, it was to unload about Officer Larry Avrech and get him off her back. For Larry, it was to dump the accusations against Lt. Black.

Donna won.

In August 1984, Donna went to Officer Avrech's immediate superior, Sergeant Harold Goudarzi. She allegedly accused Avrech of sexual harassment. She wrote this to her brother in a letter. She gave a telling interview to the "San Diego Union" that she reported Avrech "because he continuously demanded sexual favors from her and threatened to report Lieutenant Black's relationship with her to the department." Donna Gentile said, "I liked the lieutenant and didn't want to see his career harmed because of me."

Sergeant Goudarzi had to report Donna's accusations to those above him, and Internal Affairs commenced their investigation of Officer Larry Avrech. To try and save his butt, Avrech alleges he told IA that he wasn't harassing Donna, but was trying hard to gain her confidence. When pressed, Officer Avrech explained how he was trying to pull together evidence that would implicate Lieutenant Black's activity with prostitutes. IA instructed Avrech to lay off of Gentile. In the investigation, Larry admitted to writing the letter in support of Donna for her sentencing hearing, but he flatly denied having sex with her or giving her inside information of when vice was becoming aggressive against hookers.

Donna's accusations against Avrech and the subsequent investigation of Avrech's activities opened up a can of worms. No matter if the Colorado River trip was some kind of "understanding" in the department, the official inquiries forced Internal Affairs to start an investigation of Lieutenant Black.

Donna brought her complaint against Avrech in August 1984. Events quickly moved forward from there. The department suspended Avrech in January 1985. By June 1985, there would be investigations, appeals, several courtroom proceedings, fired cops, and Donna would be dead.

To All Personnel..............Division: Eastern..........January 15, 1985
San Diego Police Department
Avrech's Suspension Letter:

Officer Larry Avrech I.D. # 2900 has been suspended from duty pending investigation effective this date. Until further notice he is under orders not to be within or on the grounds of any San Diego Police Department Facility unless escorted by an on-duty San Diego Police Department Supervisor nor is he to be allowed entry to such facilities by anyone unless so escorted. Your cooperation is appreciated.

R.J. Seden, Lieutenant

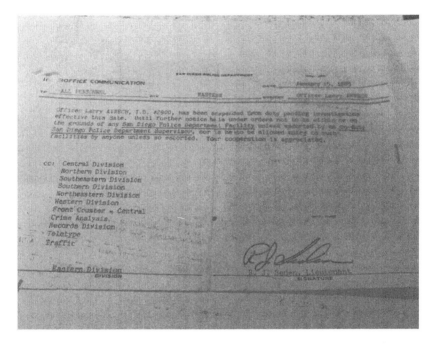

Avrech's Suspension Letter.

9

Everything Unravels For Everybody

onna lodging a formal complaint against Officer
Larry Avrech started a house of cards tumbling
down that had far-reaching and tragic conclusions.
In the ten months between going to the police about Avrech
and her death in June 1985, a great deal occurred. It affected
Donna, Avrech, and Black personally, and focused the type
of publicity on the police department that they would rather
avoid.

The immediate result of Donna's harassment complaint
against Larry Avrech was that the police department pun-
ished both Lt. Black and him. The San Diego cops did do a
fairly thorough investigation, and the conclusions they
arrived at forced them to fire both officers, but Black was
later reinstated. I do not think it would be too far-fetched
to believe that the department was relieved to punish Larry

Avrech while they might have regretted doing the same to Lieutenant Black. How the two were dealt with shows the bias in the department between the two men.

The police force let go of Avrech based on Donna's claims that he had sex with her in exchange for him updating her on when and where any vice squad crackdowns were taking place, which was confidential police information. She also confessed that Avrech did write a letter for her where he asked the judge to go easy on her for her 1984 conviction on prostitution charges. In Donna's telling of how it went down, she alleged that Larry wrote the letter to the judge, gave her fifty dollars, and then wanted sex for all that he just did. Donna allegedly continued her statement by saying that she refused and that Avrech began a steady campaign of sexually harassing her and threatened her whenever he could. She told us all of what was going on and her fears.

In response to Donna's complaint, Officer Larry Avrech steadfastly stated that he did not harass her but was trying to win her over so he could obtain the information and evidence that he needed to bring charges against Lieutenant Carl Black. Larry had to admit to the letter he wrote to the judge, but he flatly denied that he either gave her money or demanded sex. Larry further denied giving her any information about anything the police were doing, especially as it pertained to crackdowns on prostitutes.

That was enough for the department to get rid of Avrech. Lt. Black got pulled into the scandal when Larry talked about the Colorado River trip and everything he knew or suspected Black of doing with a prostitute. Internal Affairs had no choice but to open an investigation on Black and see where it would take them. I don't blame Larry for wanting justice, but this could have been handled in a more thought-out approach. I suspect Internal Affairs saw an opportunity and tied this scandal in with the informant work Donna was doing to cover up and this made Avrech look like a bad guy.

As details came out about the trip and Black's participation, the department decided that it fit the definition for fraternization with a prostitute, which was a direct violation of police department rules. For that, the force gave Black a ten-day suspension.

The firing came later as the investigation further uncovered that Carl Black had co-signed Donna Gentile's bail bond and had reached out to the probation department to try and sway its sentencing of Donna for her 1984 prostitution conviction. Both of these actions fell under the department's description of conduct unbecoming an officer. Deputy city attorney Nina Deane called Gentile a "manipulator" and said that she used Lt. Black.

Panel told demoted policeman was naive

By Dick Weber
Staff Writer

Former San Diego police Lt. Carl Black, who nearly lost his job but was demoted instead for contacting a probation officer on behalf of a prostitute, was portrayed yesterday as naive and an individual who did the right thing.

The descriptions were given at a city Civil Service Commission hearing on Black's appeal to get back his lieutenant's bar. The three-member panel took the case under advisement, but a spokesman said a decision will not be issued for several weeks.

Black told the commissioners his only interest was in rehabilitating

when the phone call to the probation officer was discovered, but Black appealed to Police Chief Bill Kolender and the action was modified to demotion to sergeant.

The investigation concluded no illicit relationship existed between Gentile and Black and that he was motivated solely to trying to change her lifestyle.

Deputy city attorney Nina Deane yesterday said Black "had good intentions," but contended rehabilitation was not an appropriate job for a police lieutenant.

Deane called Gentile "a manipulator. She was somebody who used him." Gentile, the commission was told, had five prior prostitution con-

"I think he's getting a bad deal," Gillette said.

While three top police officials who investigated Black's case said yesterday it was well known in the department that contacting a probation officer was against regulations, a police captain testified he saw nothing wrong with the phone call.

The captain said, however, Black should have first cleared the call with his superior.

Black's attorney, Ed Dillon, argued an officer's career was being ruined because of a phone call. He said there is no evidence to support the contention that the department was discredited.

In addition to deciding Black

Soon after the department fired him, Carl Black approached Police Chief Bill Kolender who reinstated Black to the force but demoted him to sergeant. The stipulation was that if Sergeant Black kept his nose clean and performed well for a year, he would be eligible to regain his lieutenant's rank. Both Black and Avrech launched an appeal on the disciplinary actions leveled against them to the Civil Service Commission.

I believe how the police department treated Avrech and Black clearly illustrates how working for the San Diego cops was not a level playing field. If the department liked you, they took care of you. If they looked at you as a troublemaker or a malcontent, you were left to fend for yourself. Avrech was not held in high esteem from almost his first day on the force, and it probably made more than one cop happy he was gone.

I have to think that Donna never saw that charging a complaint against Avrech would cause Lt. Black to lose his position on the force. His efforts helped her obtain the work furlough program when the judge sentenced her, but she didn't know that yet. To her, she was facing jail, and she was losing hold of the people she thought could help her. For all she knew, she was going to prison for anywhere from three to six months, and it scared her. She had already retained attorney Douglas Holbrook on March 7, 1984. When Donna expressed to Holbrook before all this that she knew law enforcement that could do her favors, Holbrook encouraged her to utilize her resources. Also she was advised by August Anderson, a legal source at Holbrook's office whom Donna rode horses with, not to go forward, but Donna did anyway. Attorney Holbrook became more than Donna's lawyer for the short time he represented her. As with most people, Holbrook liked her and wanted the best for his client. They struck up as much of a friendship as a client and attorney could have, and Holbrook helped provide Donna with moral support in situations where he was not representing her. Donna expressed to Holbrook that she feared retaliation, and she feared Avrech. She even put those fears in a letter to the family. She never feared Black. Sometimes your best friends are your enemies.

One of Donna's last cards she held was the work she was doing for Internal Affairs as an informant. The rather sketchy agreement she worked out with IA is that she wore a wire while meeting with members of law enforcement so Internal Affairs could record the conversations taking place. In exchange, the police department agreed to help her out with the pending appeal of her prostitution conviction. I say the agreement was "sketchy" because Douglas Holbrook found the department's offer of assistance ambiguous. According to him, the details of the who and what Donna would be informing on was never made clear.

Donna and attorney Douglas Holbrook.

The details of Donna's role as an Internal Affairs informant are very murky. There is no timeline of the investigations they had her perform. They called her when they needed her and she was paid per diem. As a police informant reporting on cops, Donna was putting herself in a dangerous predicament. It was getting to the point that she didn't only have jail to worry about, but she had a genuine concern for the safety of her life!

The job she took on with IA was perilous for a girl in her position. Helping to bring down police officers was the kind of thing that could get her killed by law enforcement. She began to fear for her life. Internal Affairs did not care about her life; they just wanted the job done. They capitalized on her looks, intelligence, and innocent appearance to put her in the middle of a sting operation. The fact that they felt a prostitute's life didn't matter was all the better for the department. She was walking on thin ice during these activities, and the cops who might have been part of IA's focus were harassing her for every little thing she did. They even threatened her by following her home on several occasions. Internal Affairs promised to relocate her, and they did put a deadbolt on her door for more security, but that was not enough.

Douglas Holbrook was aware of corruption within the department, but he and Donna were largely in the dark about what Internal Affairs was trying to find out through Donna's role as an informant. They had no clue about the investigations.

On March 13, 1985, after the denial of her appeal for the prostitution conviction, Donna began serving her ninety-day sentence at the Las Colinas Detention Facility as part of the work furlough program. She ended up doing 53 of the 90 days. Before she went to jail, she received publicity on the news and in the newspapers with regards to the firing of Black and Avrech. She feared for her life and expressed it in a letter. "I'm scared. Avrech is crazy." But she also feared that Black was angry. In this crucial disturbing letter, she expressed the danger she was facing. She also blamed herself, just as a scared, vulnerable woman would do. Donna was ahead of the times in 1985, asserting her rights, when she alleged being sexually harassed by Officer Avrech in a time when women didn't use that verbiage as they do today in the modern world, and she even underlines that her life is in danger when she gets out of jail. She also made the recorded tape that she gave to her lawyer as you will read later. There was so much going on by this point it all lumped together her friendship with Officer Avrech and Lt. Black that she got fired along with her police informant duties. Ultimately Donna was caught between the power of two men, one who cared for her; Lt. Black and the other one she feared; Officer Avrech. Her fear led to the betrayal of her dear friend, Lt. Black, a betrayal she never intended.

Black did not have to give her money and gifts, but I believe there was a true fondness there.

Donna Gentile Inmate # 85-121-645
Las Colinas Detention Facility
9000 Cottonwood Ave.
Santee, Ca. 92071

An excerpt from Donna while in Jail
April 2, 1985

I also been on the news here and in the papers for about a week because I turned in a cop in to internal affairs because he was sexually harassing me. The cop knew I turned him in.I was very scared because he's crazy. They put a dead bolt on my door and offered to relocate me, internal affairs said they would do everything they could to keep me out of jail, because what I was doing for them and the pressure it was on me. They didn't do nothing for me.. I went to the news the day before I went to jail. There was another officer who was trying to help me-he was a Lieutenant- the other officer knew he gave me money and tried to help me, so I told internal affairs, unfortunately he went down with him. The news made it look like I was out to get a cop and said what I was doing for a living, before I went to the news the cop was fired after they completed their investigation. The Lieutenant got a 10 day suspension.. I've talked to the Lieutenant after this, he is still my friend, the news made him look just as bad and the department fired him because of the news pressure. I feel so bad about this, but there's nothing I can do.

Everybody thinks my life is in danger here when I get out. Lieutenant was a good cop he had a lot of rank, I don't think he knows why I did this, he's probably very angry, everyone tells me to leave town right away, I would come back but my horse means so much to me, I just can't give her up. I would have to figure a way to bring her.

DONNA GENTILE 85-131-645
c/o LAS COLINAS DETENTION FACILITY
9000 COTTONWOOD AVE.
SANTEE, CA, 92071   APRIL 2, 1985

I also been on the news here and in the papers for about a week, because I turned a cop in to INTERNAL AFFAIRS because he was sexually HARASSING ME. The cop new I turned him in. I was very scared because he's crazy

Page 2

Bust on my door and ask to relocate me.
Internal Affairs said they would do everything
they could to keep me out of jail, because
what I was doing for them and the pressure it
was on me, they didn't do nothing for me.
I went to the News the day before I went
to jail, there was another officer who was
trying to help me he was a Lutint, the
other officer knew he (Lutint) gave me money
and tryed to help me so he told Internal
Affairs, unfortunly he went down with him
the News made it look like I was out to get
a cop and said what I was doing for a
living, before I went to the News the cop
was fired after they completed their investigation. The Lutint got ten day suspension.
I've talk to T after this he was still my
friend, the News made him look just as
bad, and the department fired him because
of the News pressure, I feel so bad about
this, but theres nothing I can do. Everybody
thinks my life is in danger when I get out
Lutint was a good cop he just ain't of Rank
I don't think he knows why I did this, he's
probably very angry, everyone tells me to leave
Town right away, I would come back but
my horse means so much to me, I just can't
give her up. I would have to run away

INMATE # 85-121-645
DONNA MARIE GENTILE
LAS COLINAS WOMENS DETENTION:
Time Served: March 13, 1985 to May 5, 1985

Donna entered the Las Colinas San Diego Detention
Facility, which is a jail specifically for women. This was
Donna's new home for the next 53 days. On arrival, the
prison guards unshackled the women, including Donna,
walked them down this long hall, fingerprinted them, and
dressed them in blue prison garbs. Donna wore the navy blue

pants and shirt with the black letters "SD" on the front and back. She even had to wear jail underwear. She was given a medical exam so that nurses could winnow out the ones with drug and psychiatric problems. It is estimated that one in five inmates are mentally ill.

The nurses then repeatedly go over your charges with you to make sure that you are competent. If not, then one can become a 1368 penal code and be considered mentally incompetent and sent off to Patton State Hospital. That wasn't the case for Donna. There were all kinds of women in there for many different crimes. Donna made some friends in there, but she was treated special because she had privileges to leave every day. Work furlough is given to inmates who have good character and show good stability.

As Donna told us the story, she said that the deputies then interviewed them and reclassified the inmates and put them into a secure module or open bay. Each inmate was classified according to their medical exam and sentence. If deputies considered one a risk, then she was placed in an individual cell. Donna showed respect and had a good reputation. Jail was as good as it could get for Donna. She lived in an occupied bay with other inmates.

Donna entered the facility with trepidation and relief. Although she didn't want to be in jail, she felt relieved not to be living in fear of the cops while there. Donna's experience in jail was good and bad. The work furlough was a blessing that was put in place for her, which meant she was able to go out from 9 to 5 and seek employment at assigned agencies. She couldn't drive because she didn't have insurance. Otherwise, she would have been able to drive out daily. Her car was parked at the jail.

When she entered the jail and realized she had to stay for at least 53 days of her 90-day sentence, it was quite scary at first. The first thoughts that went through her mind were,

"If I hadn't committed a crime, I would not be here. If my life were different, I would not be here." These thoughts repeated over and over.

Donna did a lot of reflection on her past and present life. She was a wounded child. She had always been locked away, whether it was in the Tabor home for delinquent children to not being able to have contact with her real dad. It extended to living with men who expected sex from her to her life as a prostitute. She was clearly a walking prison in her own body. She expressed to the family in letters that she was going to make her way home when she found someone to haul her horse Fantasia back.

Donna called her brother every few days and cried fearfully. Since he had been living with us, I witnessed and experienced a lot of confusion as to what was really going on in her life. She cried with a sense that she knew her life was coming to an end. I only wish I could have gone there to get her. I was ready to get on a plane and pick her up after her jail time and help her get things together and bring her back home. But my intuition stopped me. I became scared, thinking that if I did that, then maybe those after her would make me a victim of murder also, similar to the OJ murders. These thoughts controlled me, and if I were stronger then and had more support, I would have gone to her rescue. I remember we kept telling her to come back as soon as possible and to leave the horse. The tension built up in our home and in our hearts. We embodied a sense of pain so deep and nowhere to go with it. We were living her life day in and day out, especially at this most dangerous time. We felt helpless, powerless, and we didn't know how to help her.

While most inmates complained that the time dragged, Donna only wished it dragged longer. She was by far the safest in jail. On May 5, 1985, Donna was released from jail only to be faced with her enemies. She was free and never wanted to do jail time again. However, she wished she could have stayed longer because she feared for her life from the cops when she was released.

Las Colinas Detention Facility.

Located in Santee, the Las Colinas Detention and Reentry Facility (LCDRF) serves as the primary point of intake for women prisoners in San Diego County. It sits in the middle of suburbia. The new facility opened in August 2014, replacing the old Las Colinas Detention Facility. That facility was built in 1967 and operated for a period as a juvenile facility before becoming a women's facility in 1979. The new facility is staffed by approximately 278 sworn employees and 143 professional staff members. With the new facility came the implementation of new operational philosophies. It's run by the county sheriff. Residents say the jail no longer belongs there in their thriving communities.

Work Furlough Program

The Work Furlough ("WF") Facility is operated by Correctional Alternatives Incorporated ("CAI"), under contract with the County of

San Diego and is located at 551 South 35th Street, San Diego, CA 92113. The WF facility houses both male and female county inmates. Work Furlough is a sentencing alternative for judges that allows an inmate to maintain employment while serving a custody commitment. The WF facility is a community-based custodial setting that provides opportunities for a WF inmate to work and interact in the community while still under custody supervision. As such, WF inmates must show maturity and stability while both in the WF facility and the community. As a participant in the Work Furlough Program, inmates will be allowed to check out of the facility to go to work. Inmates will be required to return to the facility each day as soon as the workday is completed. The majority of inmates are required to take public transportation; however, some inmates are approved to drive with proper documentation. Inmates can also attend school, religious services, and programs like SB38, First Conviction Program, Anger Management and other court-ordered counseling. Alcoholics Anonymous/Narcotics Anonymous are offered weekly on-site at the WF facility. Inmate's family and friends will be able to visit on the weekends at the WF facility.

Her last apartment was the building owned by Sheriff Charles Cono, a reserve sheriff, and a corporation. The property managers were Cono-Hankin and Asad located on El Cajon Blvd. When she went to jail, they issued an unlawful detainer for eviction. She was evicted April 3, 1985, from her Spring Street apartment in La Mesa for not paying those last three month's rent while in jail. Her friend Michelle removed and secured her belongings. She took care of her dog Bear and horse Fantasia while Lt. Black cared for her bird.

Also, at this time, Donna filed a claim against seven police officers: Sgt. Michael Blakely, officers Curtis Meyer, Richard Draper, and Robert Candland, and detectives Frank Christensen, James Brooks, and Jeffrey Dean. She reported them for harassing her to such a degree that she had no choice but to lodge the complaint. According to Holbrook, these cops issued her fifteen tickets in a short amount of time, sometimes within a few hours of each other. Donna reported to Lt. Larry Linstrom while she was an informant. Avrech and Black did not figure into this sting as she was friends with them.

Donna lived at the Spring Hill Apartments before going to jail.

Her role as an informant shook Donna. In one way, she was safer in jail at that point. As I mentioned before, cops and criminals have the same reaction to snitches. They hate them and will do what they can to shut them up or get rid of them. Donna also put herself in an untenable position with Internal Affairs while she was an informant. She eventually went back to prostitution to make ends meet. IA cannot use an active criminal as an informant, and this hampered their ability to do much for Donna.

Her attorney, Holbrook, filed a claim against the city seeking undermined damages on March 14, 1985, because she suffered such emotional distress from the work she did as an informant. He later filed a second action, which was still pending when Donna died.

Gentile filed city claim accusing 7 cops

On May 5, 1985, Donna was released from jail. She moved in with a family that befriended her. They were her girlfriend Michele's family. Michele Tennies was the one who watched, stabled, and took care of her dear horse, Fantasia. Donna rented a room from Michele's parents in the North Park neighborhood of San Diego. She began working a security job that was in place for her from 10:00 p.m. to 6:00 a.m. Her last job was with Timmins security.

Donna was anxious about getting started in her new life and hoped to get back to the East Coast one day. California is spread out and full of transplants. It is a challenging state to build roots in, and just as challenging to leave. She had her horse and bird, a true animal lover she was. She also had a new boyfriend named John Romano, originally from New York. Things were looking up. She wrote in a letter to her brother that he wanted to marry her, but she wasn't ready to marry an ardent new boyfriend. She had dreams of living the normal life and coming back home to the east coast to be close to her family and rebuild the relationship with her mother. But this dream died!

So many people told her to get out of town. They thought Donna was crazy to stay in San Diego after what happened to Avrech and Black. People she had been close with did not have sympathy for her, as they thought she was out to get the cops and that she was a snitch. The department's actions forced this label on her. The ones who wanted her to leave town thought her life was in danger. Since she couldn't afford to transport her horse, she stayed. She found peace and love in this horse and to leave her behind would be to leave a part of herself behind.

Larry Avrech (left) with his attorney.

On May 16, 1985, Larry Avrech's hearing with the Civil Service Commission took place. His attorney Donald S. Peterson set this up. Larry was 32 then. It was about him wanting to keep his job, and he wanted to tell how the police had treated him unfairly. Avrech, as he showed during his other difficulties while employed with the police department, wasn't going quietly. He believed he was unfairly singled out and persecuted for things that other cops did. He even went to the producers of the television newsmagazine show "60 Minutes" to try and draw interest to his story.

At this point, the chip on Larry Avrech's shoulder was

the size of a log. He felt that everyone should know of his story and the truth be told. He would single-handedly show all that was wrong with the San Diego Police Department and that he would be vindicated. He truly felt that there were double standards in the police department. While this was certainly true, it seemed like it was one set of standards for him, and one for everyone else. Maybe it was ego; maybe it was disillusionment. Whatever the case, Larry would get his job back and others would have to suffer the consequences of what they did to him, but it didn't work out that way.

Donna on the witness stand.

At the hearing, Donna was called as a witness since her jail time was over. In fact, she was the star witness. Attorney Holbrook accompanied her to the hearing. He had no status as an attorney there because Donna wasn't on trial, but he was there to hold her hand and support her. When they arrived, they were surprised to see television cameras there. After all, this was a local Civil Service Commission hearing.

Though he denies it, I suspect that Larry Avrech or his attorney arranged to have the news cameras at the hearing or perhaps IA did. Since it was posted in the papers, the press could have gotten wind of it and just showed up. "60 Minutes" had rebuffed him, and he believed his case was bigger than it was. He did have an inflated opinion of his importance in the entire scenario, and due to his efforts, the hearing ended up seen throughout the country via different news reports. In a situation that would often repeat in our days of 24/7 news, something that would normally be in the local San Diego newspapers for a couple of days became a much bigger story. If something really isn't news, then with a little effort, you can make it big news.

At the hearing, Donna was dressed in business attire: a blue suit with a white lace cut blouse swooned with pearls that Avrech allegedly claims Internal Affairs bought for her for the occasion. From IA's viewpoint, they wanted to appear sound in their investigation and conclusions concerning Officer Larry Avrech. Any hearing can be as much style as it is substance and if Internal Affairs aimed for Donna to appear as the innocent "girl next door," they succeeded.

During the hearing, Donna repeated the details of her contact and relationships with Officer Avrech and Lt. Black. She continued to state that she and Black never had a sexual component to their relationship.

Sergeant Goudarzi, Avrech's supervisor when he was on the vice detail, testified on Avrech's behalf. He called out Donna's credibility as a witness. It was almost that old, "Well, she's a prostitute. You can't believe her" rationalization. What he did say was that she was a "troublemaker and a known complainer." He said at the hearing, "She didn't like the idea we weren't allowing her to work."

When all was said and done, the police filed no additional disciplinary or criminal charges against Avrech for allegedly having sex with Donna. It seemed that the police department's decision to not slap Avrech with additional charges for alleged sexual misconduct was because they found his testimony on that part of the charges were more credible than Donna's allegations. However, his dismissal from the San Diego Police Department would stay for violating police department policies. These included giving confidential information to Donna, trying to influence a judge on her behalf, and conducting an inappropriate personal relationship with her.

While Donna's alleged accusations of sexual harassment against Avrech didn't hold up, everything else that came to light did. The police department was finished with Avrech. While his attempts at grandstanding at the hearing brought a great deal of attention to him, I would have to think that it backfired on him when the Civil Service Commission upheld most of the original charges. If he was the one who had called in the television cameras, what he thought would be a brilliant stroke toward vindication only meant that a great many more people than just a few interested parties in San Diego knew about him.

One of the items that came to light during this hearing is that more people now knew Donna was a police informant and a prostitute. Again, on a local level, some people in and out of the police department knew this, but it became a widespread fact due to the news cameras. One thing you want more than anything when you are a snitch is anonymity.

Donna already feared for her life because of her informant's role. Now many people knew about what she did.

Donna was very effective and compelling during the hearing. Enough of what she said sustained the original decision for the police department to fire Avrech. Carl Black had his hearing coming up in a couple of weeks. He must have wondered if Donna would be just as effective during that hearing and where it would lead for him. Even though Donna had stuck up for him at Avrech's hearing, Black had to be apprehensive when it was his turn. Keeping in mind IA put the pressure on the 22-year-old.

He didn't have to find out. In about two weeks after Avrech's hearing was done and his firing upheld, and two days before Black's hearing, Donna Gentile was found dead. Go figure!

S.D. police lieutenant in vice case to be demoted, not fired

By Dick Weber
Staff Writer

The San Diego Police Department has reversed its decision to fire a police lieutenant for allegedly having an inappropriate relationship with a prostitute and instead will demote him to sergeant.

Carl Black, 40, who was fired last month after 16 years on the force, appealed his discharge directly to Chief Bill Kolender. Kolender assigned the case to Assistant Chief conduct was becoming.

"Beyond that I don't want to comment, because we've got a hearing coming up."

A police internal affairs investigation concluded that Black had an "inappropriate relationship" last year with 22-year-old Donna Gentile, who is serving a three-month jail term on a prostitution conviction. A second San Diego police officer, Larry Avrech, was fired as part of the internal investigation involving

Police officer fired in prostitution case

By Jerry K. Remmers and Joe Hughes
Tribune Staff Writers

Police administrators said today they have fired one officer and are recommending dismissal of a lieutenant in connection with a probe of allegations of improper conduct involving a woman described as a prostitute.

Assistant Police Chief Bob Burgreen said two other officers have been cleared of allegations which involved information brought to the department by Donna Gentile, 22.

Burgreen said state law prohibits him from releasing the names of the officers involved.

However, police sources said they are Patrolman Larry Avrech, who was fired, and Lt. Carl Black, who has a hearing scheduled before Deputy Police Chief Norman Stamper Monday. Burgreen said the recommendation to Stamper is that the officer be fired.

Gentile, in a television interview last night, also named Avrech and Black as the officers involved.

Burgreen said Gentile was interviewed at length during the department's six-month internal investigation and is a police witness in the case.

She has alleged that officers paid to have sex with her, had traffic tickets fixed, helped keep her out of jail on prostitution charges by writing a favorable letter to a judge, and took her on an all-expenses-paid vacation to the Colorado River.

Burgreen said he was upset that a television station yesterday displayed the photograph of one of the officers who was cleared by the department.

Gentile alleged that Black had co-signed her $1,000 bail when she was arrested one of six times last summer after police conducted sweeps against prostitution along El Cajon Boulevard.

The program eventually led to the arrest of 363 prostitutes and customers, and more than 3,000 people were contacted by officers during the sweep.

Burgreen said investigators confirmed that an officer had signed the woman's bail in violation of department policy.

As a result of the television interview, Burgreen said he is also seeking information on a possible reserve officer the woman knew only as "Mike." She said she had sex with him three times in or near Las Colinas Women's Detention Center.

The officers involved in the probe are members of the department's Eastern Division vice detail and were responsible for combating prostitution along El Cajon Boulevard, police sources said.

10

The Body On Sunrise Highway

Donna's body was found on Sunday, June 23, 1985. The last person that seemed to have seen Donna alive, according to the police, was her landlord. This was one of Michelle's parents, the ones who let Donna stay at their home after she got out of jail. It was on Utah Street in San Diego. They were helping her out until she was back on her feet. When Donna never came home, Michelle's parents called the police. She had obtained the security job while on the work-furlough program at the jail. She never made it into work that day. It is unclear whether she had left behind her prostitute's life at that point. As we will see, a great deal was unclear about the end of Donna's life and still is today.

Information is scarce if the police or any of her friends that knew of her disappearance made any effort to find her. After all, when she was active being a prostitute, there were times when sightings of Donna were scarce because she would be with a client somewhere. Looking back, I don't know if Donna was hooking at the time. She just got out of jail. Even on the work-furlough program, jail was an experience she didn't want to do again. She had a boyfriend, she had a job, she had some good friends, and she had her horse. She seemed to be the type of girl who would learn from an experience like going to jail. She wasn't a fan of being a prostitute; it was just a means to an end. Now she could once again try to reboot her life.

Donna's body dead, pebbles stuffed in her mouth.

The reboot never got very far. A man was walking his dog along the Sunrise Highway when he came across the body on that Sunday morning. The section of the highway where he found her was thirty miles east of San Diego County, so it was not the San Diego Police Department that answered the call, but rather the San Diego County Sheriff's Department. They conducted the murder investigation where she was discovered nude on the embankment of a vehicle turnoff on

Sunrise Highway in San Diego County. The location of the road is in the rugged rural eastern portion of San Diego, approximately 34 miles from 70th Street and El Cajon where Donna usually worked her prostitution gig. She was discovered in the underbrush near a highway exit ramp in a remote mountain area known as Mt. Laguna.

Mt. Laguna, San Diego County.

When the first car arrived on the scene, the officers found Donna's naked body on the ground face up with her clothes piled on top of her body. The clothing was cut on the side from the bottom up along the seams in a seductive manner which seemed unusual. Her pantyhose were dumped to the side on the ground next to her body. The pantyhose were sent to the FBI in Quantico where they scraped it for forensic evidence such as hair and fiber. Several fibers were recovered including a tan wool fiber and acrylic fibers that were consistent with fibers found on sheepskin seat covers.

Body identified as call girl linked to police

By Homer Clance
Staff Writer

A nude body found near the Sunrise Highway on June 23 was identified yesterday as that of Donna Marie Gentile, 22, a prostitute involved in the firing of one San Diego police officer and the demotion of another.

Deputy coroner Dan Matticks said identification was made through fingerprints on file with authorities.

Former police officer Larry Avrech, 32, a five-year veteran, was fired based on accusations that he had an improper relationship with Gentile and furnished her confidential information that helped her avoid arrests for prostitution.

Lt. Carl Black, 40, a 18-year veteran, was demoted to sergeant for his relations with Gentile. According to testimony at his Civil Service appeals hearing, Black contacted a probation officer on behalf of Gentile and gave her $1,000 toward legal expenses for her arrest.

Gentile, who has several arrests and convictions for prostitution, was a key witness at the appeals hearings for Avrech and Black.

Matticks said that Gentile had been beaten about the head and strangled.

Her body was found in brush about 360 feet west of Sunrise Highway, about two miles north of Interstate 8, he said.

There was one yellow earring on the ground next to her. It had two yellow metal strips on a white background with yellow metal on the reverse side. The other was missing. Later, they searched her car and apartment for clues. The area was roped off for proper forensic procedures to be followed at the crime scene. Police took photos, and the area was swept for any clues that might lead to a better understanding of what happened. The information gathered that day points to very little being found at the scene. Jeff Dean was the officer at the scene of her murder.

Donna's death was particularly brutal. She certainly suffered at the hand of her murderer or murderers. It was not an easy way to go. She was beaten around the head, strangled, and suffered a probable bite mark. Numerous fractures appeared around her neck and along her back. She also had gravel stuffed in her mouth. In all probability, the neck and back fractures occurred when she was being held down and her mouth held open with some kind of instrument while the gravel and dirt were poured down her mouth. With the neck fractures, an instant paralysis occurred. When the cervical 2 area is snapped, it causes an inability to move. Even if she wanted to fight back and defend herself, she couldn't.

While her autopsy has been locked away to this very day, some facts came out about her death. She was still alive when her mouth was stuffed with the gravel. The official cause of death was asphyxiation, as the garbage they shoved in her mouth went down her throat and choked off her cricoid cartilage, which is the primary airway. Deputy Coroner Dan Matticks gave the official explanation of her death as "manual strangulation and airway obstruction by foreign material." Whatever the description, it was a terrible way for a young woman to die. There is a good chance that Donna had to be looking into the eyes of her killer as her life ebbed away.

There is a good argument for there being more than one killer at the scene. Her bruises and fractures show that somebody had to be holding her down and beating her. Donna wasn't a big girl, only 5'4" in height, and one strong man could have done all of this to her. However, two people there make a lot of sense, especially when you consider the scenario of someone holding her down while the gravel was being forced into her mouth.

Former Bucks woman found dead in Calif.

A former Bucks County woman has been found strangled in a remote, mountainous region near San Diego.

The body of Donna Gentile, 22, a former Levittown resident, was identified July 3 through fingerprint records, authorities said. Passers-by found the body lying in underbrush June 23 off a highway exit ramp 30 miles east of San Diego.

Ms. Gentile was found naked with her clothing piled nearby, and had been badly beaten before she died, authorities said.

A San Diego County sheriff's office spokesman said investigators were pursuing numerous leads in the case, but he declined to provide more specifics.

Ms. Gentile, a Philadelphia native, moved to Bucks County when she was about 11 and attended schools in Penndel Borough and Middletown and Falls townships before moving to San Diego around 1980, according to school officials, family and friends.

Family members still in this area will hold private funeral services when Ms. Gentile's remains are returned here, possibly this weekend.

Another fact that came to light was that Donna had cocaine in her system. It could have been something she took on her own before meeting the person who killed her, or it was something he gave her. Cocaine could have made her more docile and unaware of what was happening. Like many people her age, Donna dabbled in drugs now and then, but she was no addict by any means. According to the coroner report, her last meal consisted of Chinese food. The probable bite mark on her neck area could have been the remnants of a scar or from her attacker.

Forensic samples collected from Donna's body by SDPD criminalist M.L. Pierson showed ABO blood. Swabs done on her buttocks tested positive for semen and saliva. Semen was also found in the vagina, but there weren't any spermatozoa in the semen. This brings up the question of whether she had sex with someone before she met up with the killer or did it belong to the killer?

Methods for getting more information from such evidence were not as sophisticated in 1985 as they do now. DNA testing regarding a crime was only developed in 1984. It was in its infancy at that time and took a few more years to become an acceptable part of processing a crime scene. If Donna's death happened today, investigators might have had more solid evidence to go on, but more about that in the next chapter.

There was nothing of importance found at the crime scene. Donna's pocketbook and any identification were not found at the crime scene. In fact, none of it ever turned up. It was San Diego Police Officer Jeff Dean who identified her body. Once authorities knew who she was, they knew where to go to search her room and her car. Besides her ID never being found, there was very little investigators could find out about what had happened to Donna.

The fact that there wasn't much to be determined from

the crime scene was actually enlightening in its own way. The area seemed to be swept clean of any possible clues before the police got there. Any possible footprints or tire tracks were brushed away. It looked like the area was sterilized by someone who had a good idea of police procedures. This meant a rather experienced criminal or someone in the police department.

Another detail is that she had been dead for at least 24 hours. Not a lot has been gleaned in the almost 35 years since her death on anything that happened on that weekend in June.

One of the most interesting facts of her murder is the gravel that killed Donna. In the world of organized crime, a dead body with stones or dirt shoved into the mouth was the sign that the victim was a snitch. It is kind of ironic that the two organizations that couldn't stand snitches are the mob and a police department. The mob you can understand. If somebody snitches on what they are doing, then the members of the mob have a better chance of going to jail. The police, on the other hand, can have this "we can do no wrong" mentality that can be punctured with one person telling the public about what really goes on.

Whoever killed Donna in this manner knew what he was trying to show by the way he killed her. Exactly what Donna said about a person and in what context is not known. If we did, it would certainly help narrow the field of suspects. There is a chapter coming up where I present thoughts on who might have killed Donna and why.

It took two weeks after she was found before Donna's death was made public. It is suspicious why a lid was kept on her murder. About a week before her death was announced, the Civil Service Commission came to its decision regarding their investigation into Officer Avrech and Lieutenant Black's appeals. The commission did not allow Avrech to return to the police force. He was done as a cop and would not be reinstated to the police department. While the commission acknowledged there wasn't any evidence indicating that Avrech had sex with Donna, it still maintained seven of the police department's dozen charges made against him.

One of these charges was that Avrech interfered with the department's investigation of his case and that he shared how the department was going to enforce its prostitution laws with Donna. The Commission's take on this part of the charges against Avrech also had the effect of making Donna's alleged sexual harassment charges against him not have much validity.

Lieutenant Black fared much better in the Commission's decision. It did uphold Black's demotion and placed him on probation for a year. This meant that if Black did his job well and kept his nose clean during the probationary period, he would get his former position back. This is exactly what happened as the Commission ruled that Black had nothing but good intentions when he went to the probation department on Donna's behalf. Based on things that Deputy City Attorney Nina Deane said to the Commission at the hearing, the Commission gave Black the benefit of the doubt. She told the group that Donna was a "manipulator" and was using Black. She portrayed Black as someone who was naïve and that he believed everything Donna told him.

As soon as Avrech's last hearing was over, the newspapers were full of news about Donna's death. It was July 3, 1985, weeks after her actual death. You didn't have to be a conspiracy theorist to read between the lines of reporters' stories. Larry Avrech could be looked at as someone who wanted to get rid of Donna for his own gain. It could be argued that her alleged harassment charges are what led to his ouster from the police department. Of course, anybody in that position would want revenge. The news stories about

Donna's death could certainly lead somebody to that conclusion.

Avrech later sued the San Diego Police Department for intentional infliction of emotional stress. He also tried to get Congress to launch an investigation of corruption in the San Diego Police Department. Donna was a murder victim. Avrech became a victim of police corruption and Donna's murder. It seems just a little too convenient that her murder and his final departure from the police department happened at the same time.

As for my family, two detectives from the San Diego office came to our house to tell us the heartbreaking news of Donna's death. Her brother Lou had shared some of her letters and what they talked about on the phone with some of the family. We had an idea of the type of life she was leading and what she was going through in San Diego. We had tossed around ideas at times to enable her to come back east, but nothing ever quite worked out. Today, she would have had all the social media outlets to keep in touch with her family across the country. Now, it can seem that a person three thousand miles away only lived over in the next town. Back in the early 1980s, all you had were phone calls and letters.

Donna was very selective with whom she shared information. When the news came to us, Donna's mother – my Aunt Ellen – had no clue she had been a prostitute. Whenever she wrote her mother, it was all the good things that happened. She would share about getting a job as a security guard, or a new boyfriend, or news about her horse. She would never tell her mother about her life as a prostitute. I imagine she was still hoping for that motherly love and acceptance to show up in her heart.

Assembling the material for this book has not been easy due to the time it took place and how many years have elapsed. Back in the early 1980s, it was easy to stay below the radar.

There was such a thing as privacy, and everything a person did wasn't immediately broadcast to the world or hiding in cyberspace just waiting to be found. There were many times as I tried to gather information on Donna's time in San Diego that I wished this had been in modern times. Pulling things out of old newspaper reports, public information, and scholarly research on Donna's case was about all there was to go on. Having access to Donna's letters and her conversations with her brother Lou was very important to color in the lines of the picture the news stories drew about Donna.

Nothing I can say can give you an idea of what it was like to receive that visit from the FBI to tell us that she had been murdered. It was a painstaking moment that would haunt us forever. As far as we knew at that point, Donna was out of jail and working at getting her life together. There had been talk that she and her boyfriend would actually head east for good, complete with Donna's horse. It never happened, and none of the family had seen Donna since she ran away.

It is bad enough when a relative dies and you knew it was coming. It is ter-

Our Lady of Grace Cemetery, Langhorne, Penn.

rible when it happens unexpectedly. Murder is the worst. Somebody came and took your relative's life for no good reason. People don't have the right to take another's life. It is such a violation of someone you love. Donna certainly didn't deserve to die so young, especially in the way she did. It is horrible to contemplate that someone regarded Donna as such a threat that she had to be eliminated. It took a long time for much of the family to wrap their heads around everything that occurred concerning Donna's death. We are still doing it all these years later.

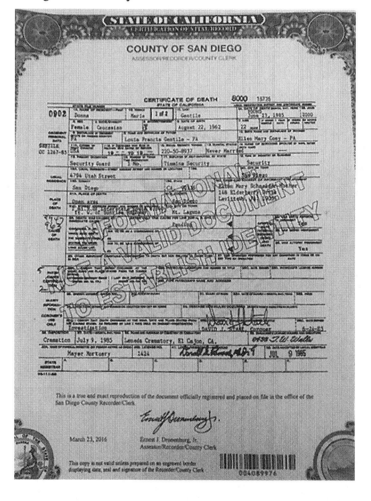

At the time we were told of Donna's murder, my Uncle Frank flew out to San Diego to bring her body back to Philadelphia. She was cremated at Leneda Crematory in El Cajon, California, and finally came back east, but there was no closure at all. The family buried her ashes at Our Lady of Grace Cemetery in Langhorne, Penn. It seems like back then we thought the investigation would quickly find out who killed Donna. When you watch enough movies and television, we all think that every case takes only a couple of days to close. Much to our further agitation and heartache, not only was the killer not found quickly but is still out there, if he or they are still alive. The investigation moved at a snail's pace. To us, she was family, and I fondly thought of the little girl I used to see when we got together. To the police, she was a prostitute, which means that no full-out investigation was warranted.

In the remaining chapters, we will take a look at what was done as an investigation after Donna's death, and look at some theories about who killed her and why she died. Finally, we will look at how Donna's death sparked a woman's movement that has grown today. The current "Me Too" movement has certain roots in what happened back in the '80s.

While the remaining chapters do not have any definitive answers about Donna's death, it is all part of her story. My intent with this book is to share the life of one young woman who learned what she had to do to survive, but whose life was cut short before she could rise above it all. If anyone gains any insight from what happened that is not recorded here, please feel free to share. Finding Donna's killer might be the only way to put what happened to rest.

THE LIFE AND MURDER OF AN INNOCENT RUNAWAY

OFFICE OF THE CORONER TOXICOLOGY REPORT

DONNA MARIE GENTILE

DATE OF DEATH: 6-23-85

CASE # 1267-85

SPECIMAN SUBMITTED: Blood (Pleural Space) Brain, Vaginal, Oral, Rectal Swabs, Liver, Bile, Kidney, Lung Vitreous Tumor, Heart, Gastric Content

ANALYSIS REQUESTED: Routine Homicide Screen

SPECIMEN SUBMITTED BY: R.V. Bucklin M.D. Examining Room

7-31-85 REPORT

Blood Drug Screen

•	Ethyl Alcohol, GLC	.01 I w/v
•	Barbiturates RIA	Not Detected
•	Phencyclidine, RIA	Not Detected
•	Cocaine/Cocaine Metabolite, RIA	Detected

Liver Basic Drug Screen

•	Common Drugs, TLC	Not Detected

Opiates, RIA

•	Bile	Not Detected

Cocaine, GLC

•	Blood	Not Detected
•	Liver	Not Detected
•	Brain	Not Detected

- Kidney   Not Detected

Acid Phosphatase, ENZ

- Vaginal Swab   139 m I.U.
- Oral Swab   9 m I.U.
- Rectal Swab   9 m I.U.

Forensic samples were collected from Donna's body by San Diego Sheriffs Dept Criminalist M.L. Pierson whose findings show the following. The blood is tested three ways in the analysis, which helps with DNA.

- Victims Blood: ABO grouping -O
  ESD grouping- 1
  PGM grouping- 1
- Buttocks swab taken from Donna Marie Gentile were tested positive for semen and saliva.
- Vaginal swab taken from Donna Marie Gentile tested positive for semen and saliva. It also tested ESD group 1 and PGM group 1. The report is not specific in weather the results are from the semen or saliva.
- No spermatozoa were found in the semen.

11

Investigation

A s mentioned before, the San Diego Sheriff's Department was in charge of Donna's murder inves- tigation since her body was discovered outside of the city of San Diego. Thomas Streed was a veteran homicide investi- gator who received the case and was in charge of the murder investigation. In comments gathered from several sources, Detective Streed ran into several dif- ficulties while investigating the murder. He had issues from the beginning with evidence discovered at the

Detective Thomas Streed was in charge of the murder investigation.

crime scene and other problems he encountered during the course of the investigation.

As someone who had been around for a while and seen different murder scenes, Streed thought the crime scene of Donna's death was different than anything he had seen in any other prostitute's murder. Many times, when a prostitute is killed, it is because the killer takes a hooker to live out a certain fantasy. He engages in his fantasy, kills the girl, takes mementos of the occasion, and poses the body in a certain way to send a message to the public. Also, most murdered prostitutes are just dumped on the road or in the woods so that the killer can then move on to the next unfortunate girl.

When Streed studied Donna's crime scene, he saw none of those common similarities to other cases. For one thing, she had not been dumped out on the road. The ravine where she was found was a bit hidden. If the man and his dog hadn't been walking right on top of the area, more time might have gone by before Donna's body was found. The other factor that was different was the degree to which all footprints and tire tracks were brushed away. The perpetrator knew what clues the police looked for at a crime scene. There was also the way Donna's clothes were piled on top of her body. For a prostitute's murder, Donna's was unlike any he had seen before. The first thought Streed had was that somebody who normally went after prostitutes did not do this.

Streed came to his conclusions as a professional veteran who understood what he was looking for at a crime scene. A good investigator can determine a great deal from carefully looking over the crime area. In some cases, they can figure out some things by what wasn't at the scene. Most murders are not committed with a great deal of forethought. The majority of killings occur as spur of the moment events. It could be a moment of passion or anger. There is little thought to what ends up happening. This is the case with most murders. Few are planned out at all, let alone in detail to the degree that the killer knows to hide his tracks from the police.

The next day, Streed learned that his first hunch about this not being a routine murder of a prostitute was correct. San Diego police officer Robert Candland came up to Streed and asked him if he realized who he had, meaning the murdered girl. Candland went on to say that Streed would be in a lot of trouble if he continued the investigation and it could be the end of his career.

What Streed gathered from the conversation is any investigation into Donna Gentile's murder was going to have political overturns and not be easy, especially if he had to ask any questions of the San Diego Police Department. After all, Candland was part of the East County division in the department. He would have an idea of how the department would feel about anything that had to do with Donna.

Bob Candland knew Donna. He had been part of the 1984 special initiative against prostitution in the city, and he had given Donna a citation for breaking a minor law. He was also one of the cops named in her harassment claim against the department. Since he was on the prostitution detail, Candland had to know Lieutenant Black, who had been in charge.

While Candland cooperated in Streed's murder investigation, Streed did discover that what he thought he was going to encounter when dealing with most of the San Diego Police Department was right on target. The administrative side of the department was of little help. They wouldn't give any substantial answers to his questions and were very uncooperative.

When Streed inquired into any of Donna's activities, he felt like he ran into a brick wall. The same thing occurred when he asked for the identities of her regular customers. Anything he got out of anyone in the police department came very reluctantly. Part of the problem was the department instituted a policy that made it difficult to get answers to any of his questions. If any police officers had any information about Donna, they first had to tell their commanders who in turn would tell Internal Affairs. Internal Affairs decided whether to pass on the information to Streed's investigators.

Even Candland was ordered not to talk to Streed or anyone else in the Sheriff's Office about the murder. Things got to the point that Streed and Candland had to hold secret meetings so that Candland could give Streed any information on Donna that might help the investigation. Candland had gotten to such a point of paranoia about his superiors that he refused to send out any information over the police radio. Candland used the communications center to call his wife and provide her a code about where he would meet Streed. She would then relay that information to Streed by calling his house.

The situation between Streed and the police department got so bad that he had a lieutenant from the Sheriff's Office arrange a meeting with the police department. Streed was not getting even general information on Donna that could point his investigation in a direction.

At the meeting, Streed noticed that the police commander they met seemed surprised at the request. All Streed could figure out was that they were expecting much more direct questions about the police department's actions with Donna when all he was looking for were simple things, such as who her regular customers were. After the meeting, the police department became a little more cooperative with Streed's efforts.

At one point, a witness came forward while the investigation was going on. She claimed that she heard two people talking about committing Donna's murder. The woman was a prostitute and said an unmarked police car picked her up on El Cajon Boulevard. This was a scheduled "date" (sex for money). They drove to a motel where another man soon showed up. They were trying to figure out a way to kill Donna. Their idea was to make it look like a date gone wrong.

The witness said that one of the men took his badge and placed it on the nightstand while they made phone calls. She could see that it was from the San Diego Police Department. When pressed later, she allegedly identified the two men from photos as cops. One was a former officer, Robert Hannibal, who the department fired in 1983 for his connection with a prostitute. The witness identified the second cop as Lt. Carl Black.

Left to right: Officer Robert Hannibal and Lt. Carl Black.

When Streed found all of this out, he asked Lieutenant Black to take a lie detector test. Black said he would, but when he showed up in the room for the polygraph exam, he immediately left. Since a polygraph is not admissible evidence in court anyway, not taking the test did not prove Black had anything to do with Donna's murder. In Streed's investigation, Carl Black was a "person of interest," but there was never enough evidence to prove anything.

Soon after Donna's death, rumblings in the San Diego newspapers began publicly speculating about corruption in the city's police department. Donna's death was particularly treated as an indication of such since it came right after testifying against Avrech and immediately before Black's hearing. People began to speculate openly if the police were involved in her death. Black, Avrech and Hannibal could be the ultimate fall guys. You decide?

Throwing fuel on this fire was a tape-recorded message Donna made weeks before her death and gave it to her lawyer, Attorney Douglas Holbrook. With all that was going on, the scandal and the reporting of Avrech to IA, she feared for her life. On July 5, 1985, after her death, the San Diego news station KGTV, Bob Donley (Channel 10) played Donna's message. She predicted her own murder and said:

Donna's Exact Recorded Words

"In case I disappear somewhere or am missing, I want my lawyer to give this to the press. I have no intention of disappearing or going out of town without letting my lawyer know first. Because of the publicity that I have given a police scandal, this is the reason why I'm making this. I feel someone in a uniform with a badge can still be a serious criminal. This is the only life insurance that I have."

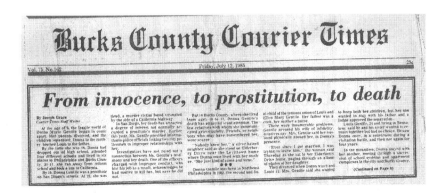

From innocence, to prostitution, to death

(Continued from Page 1)

Donna Gentile testifies at trial of police officers

Donna with her dog

There were apartments in Penndel: Middletown and Falls Township, public schools in the Neshaminy and Pennsbury districts, and Catholic schools at our Lady of Grace in Penndel and Christ the King in the Northeast.

A spokesman at one of the schools, where Donna spent three years, said no one recalled her presence. "An average kid with average grades who drifted through," he said.

Donna's mother remarried, changed her name, and moved with her daughter and husband, John Schneider, into a comfortable tan and brown Levittown home on Elderberry Drive.

But Donna began running away from home, at first for a day or so, then longer. Her father's relatives say she grew dissatisfied with life in her mother's home. Her mother and stepfather say they did all they could.

In 1977, Donna's father died. Louis Gentile said his sister told him their mother kept the death a secret from her. Her mother said she told Donna her father died and offered to take her to the funeral. Donna declined, she said.

Trouble came more swiftly then. In 1978, Donna was placed in Tabor Home, a group center for troubled children near Doylestown, for delinquency. She ran away from the home frequently, her mother said.

Louis Gentile, who had reestablished contact with his sister while she was at Tabor, said she boarded a bus with a friend in the summer of 1980, heading for California. He said she never told him why she went.

The friend returned shortly afterward. Donna stayed on, and tried to begin anew in San Diego.

There were problems from the start. Within a year of her arrival in San Diego, Donna had pleaded guilty to three counts of prostitution, but she received probation and went straight for two years, obtaining a job as a security guard, said her attorney Douglas Holbrook.

On the surface, she seemed to enjoy her new lifestyle. She sent her mother pictures of herself in her guard's uniform, a silver badge affixed to her chest. She urged her brother to join her in California.

"She said I'd never come back," Louis Gentile said.

She acquired a horse, a jet-black animal named Fantasia which she stabled in the San Diego countryside, he said. She wrote

her mother she was engaged, and sent pictures of her fiance.

But the dark cloud that shrouded Donna Gentile much of her life returned. Her engagement broke off, and she lost her guard job. Soon, she returned to the streetwalker's strip along San Diego's El Cajon Boulevard.

In 1984, she was arrested again for prostitution, her attorney said. She would eventually receive a three-month jail sentence for the offense.

But before she went to prison, Donna Gentile struck up curious relationships with two city police officers, relationships that led to the firing of one officer and the demotion of the other.

The young woman testified at civil service hearings that one officer extorted sex from her in exchange for advance warning of the time and place of police vice patrols.

She told investigators the other officer befriended her, took her on a vacation trip on the Colorado River with other officers, loaned her $1,000 to pay her legal bills, and contacted a probation officer to urge leniency on her prostitution case.

Following a series of well-publicized hearings from January through May, the officer alleged to have provided her with confidential police information was fired. The officer who urged leniency on her case was demoted for one year from lieutenant to sergeant.

On April 2, Donna wrote her brother a letter from her jail cell in which she stated she was "very scared" because she believed the officer who was fired, Larry Avrech, was "crazy."

"Everybody thinks my life is in danger when I get out," she wrote in the letter, a copy of which was obtained by the Bucks County Courier Times. "Everyone tells me to leave town right away."

She wrote that she couldn't af-

In her last letters to her mother and brother, dated June 1 and June 3, respectively, she wrote about her job and a new boyfriend who wanted to marry her. There was no hint of concern in her earlier letter.

The family with whom she was living saw her last on a Friday evening, June 21. When she did not return for several days, they notified police.

The body of an unidentified woman was found on June 23 in underbrush near a highway exit ramp in a remote, mountainous area 30 miles east of San Diego. The woman had been strangled and badly beaten, officials said.

Her neck was broken, her mouth filled with stones, according to sources close to the investigation. Using fingerprint records, coroners identified the body July 3 as that of Donna Gentile.

The body was cremated earlier this week in San Diego, family members said. Donna Gentile's remains are being flown home to Bucks County for private funeral services here Saturday.

Donna Gentile's mother said she did not know her daughter became a prostitute until after she died. At first, she refused to believe it. Now, after reading news accounts, she has come to a grudging, grieving acceptance.

Donna's brother said his sister took him 1½ years ago she had turned to prostitution out of financial desperation.

"She said she was doing it to make money to survive," Gentile said.

Gentile said he received his sister's last letter around June 8. She wrote she wasn't ready to marry an ardent new boyfriend. He said he called her to reply on June 28 — two days after her then-unidentified body was found.

"I just missed her," he said, dropping his head down.

Prostitute's death shrouded in mystery

No new leads seven months after police scandal, brutal murder

By David Hasemyer
Tribune Staff Writer

The brutal murder seven months ago of Donna Gentile, the prostitute whose association with two police officers ignited a departmental scandal, has left sheriff's homicide detectives struggling for leads. Gentile's family, angry and a former police officer contending he has been harassed by investigators who view him as a suspect.

Gentile was found dead June 23 in a Pine Valley ravine near Sunrise Highway. She had been beaten and strangled, her neck broken.

At the time of her death, the 22-year-old prostitute was embroiled in a highly publicized controversy involving two San Diego police officers.

Gentile said she was being tipped off by an officer about police enforcement activities against prostitutes along El Cajon Boulevard and that she had accompanied another officer on a trip to the Colorado River in Arizona.

After an internal police investigation, Lt. Carl Black was demoted to sergeant for one year. Black acknowledged he accompanied Gentile and a group of other officers on the river trip and paid her money to meet bail and pay

attorney's fees.

Black will be restored to the rank of lieutenant in June.

Officer Larry Avrech was fired following an investigation into Gentile's allegations that he had tipped her information about pending crackdowns on prostitution in East San Diego so she could avoid arrest.

Gentile also publicly claimed that Avrech extorted sex from her in return for information relating to police activities. Those claims, which Avrech denied, were not part of the department's charges that led to his dismissal.

Gentile told her story before a city Service Commission hearing last May in an unsuccessful appeal by Avrech for reinstatement.

A month before she was dead.

Shortly after her murder, investigators say they had recovered significant clues in the area where Gentile's body was found, in room she rented in Normal Heights and her car.

Sheriff's detectives did not promise a solution but predicted the clues send them to a suspect.

Please see GENTILE, B-3

Task force formed here on slayings

Green River Task Force is based, was strongly supportive.

Capt. Robert Evans, an original task force member and commander of the present Green River Task Force, said, "I wish them all the luck

tectives are tracking surfaced in Superior Court, at a bail review for Blake Taylor of Lemon Grove.

During the hearing, Rogers mentioned that Taylor was a suspect in at least one of the slain prostitute

the June 9 case yesterday. At one point, Rogers was asked if Taylor was a suspect in the series of slayings.

Rogers said in court that Taylor was a suspect in at least one case but

Streed continued his investigation but found nothing of any substance. The newspapers periodically lamented that lack of progress with headlines like "3 Months Later, Slaying of Prostitute Still Puzzles" and "Prostitute's Death Shrouded in Mystery" and "No New Leads Seven Months After Police Scandal" and "Brutal Murder." These articles kept the spotlight on the police department and the suspected corruption issues.

A couple of years later, a series of prostitute murders began. These "fringe women," as the police described them, soon numbered thirty-one. The San Diego Police Department and the Sheriff's Department formed a Metropolitan Homicide Task Force (MHTF) to tackle two missions: investigate the murders and police corruption. Thomas Streed was a member of the MHTF. At this point, Donna's murder, still unsolved, was made part of this task force. Even though her murder was nothing like the others, she was put under this serial murder investigation.

Streed worked with the unit for a while but was soon reassigned back to the Sheriff's Department in early 1989. The official word was that Streed went off on his own too much. However, he said in an interview with the San Diego Evening Tribune that his removal was "because he was actively investigating possible police officers' involvement in a conspiracy to kill Gentile and other police informants."

While the serial killer was eventually caught, the task force seemed more concerned with convincing the public that there was no corruption in the police department. While the department tried to pin the murder of Donna on the serial killer, the evidence wouldn't hold up, and her murder is still unofficially unsolved.

With DNA testing becoming more sophisticated by 1991, the semen found in Donna's body was tested. The results were never publicly reported. In fact, Donna's 1985 autopsy was the first to be sealed in San Diego County under an order that remains in effect to this day.

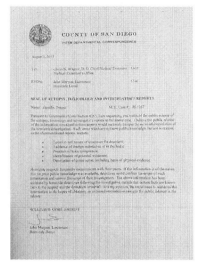 

Left: Medical Examiners Autopsy investigator report 2015

Right: KFMB-CBS-San Diego 2015, Investigative Producer David Gotfredson

As recently as 2015, Investigative Producer, David Gotfredson of CBS News 8 (KFMB) requested the San Diego County Medical Examiner to release Gentile's autopsy under the California Public Records Act. The agency issued a denial letter, which said the San Diego County Sheriff's Department wanted to keep the autopsy sealed. It said:

"Until this directive is rescinded by the investigating agency, we are unable to release any information or provide any copies of our reports regarding this case... The public interest in the release of these reports and the information contained within does not outweigh the public's interest to withhold this information as it may interfere with law enforcement's investigation and/or a successful prosecution."

The police department said at the time of the denial that there were no suspects for Donna's Murder and that there was no active investigation.

There are more holes in the investigation of Donna's murder than a block of Swiss cheese. At the time, Detective Streed seemed to do as thorough of a job as anybody could. However, he seemed to be a detective with one hand tied behind his back. The cooperation of the San Diego Police Department was sketchy at best. When some of your leading suspects or sources of information are in the police department, their "wall of silence" can be an effective deterrent. To his credit, Streed never gave up. Donna was always on his mind since he took on the case, including his time on the task force. It is telling in his interview with the San Diego Evening Tribune that he was still focused on Donna's murder while a member of that MHTF.

As we will see in the next chapter, there were suspects the police put forward as the killer of Donna, but there were holes in the theory of each suspect. Too often, it seemed like the police were trying to force a round peg into a square hole when bringing up someone's name. The theories were contrived, and the evidence was circumstantial at best. At no time did anybody in the police department come up as a suspect, except for Carl Black, Streed's person of interest.

It is a mystery to the family why the autopsy report in Donna's case is now sealed. While the DNA was analyzed in 1991, there wasn't much of a database to compare it to back then. That is not the case now. The FBI data on DNA is quite extensive. Most people arrested have to give a DNA sample now. It is kept on file for all military personnel. Other sources also bring more DNA information into the huge store of data.

Do the police periodically take the DNA information from the semen found in Donna and compare it to the current data? Let's say that Donna's murder was committed as a random act by someone who has sex with a prostitute, kills her, and then shovels gravel down the throat of his victims for fun. In no way do I think a random person like that did this, but if it were, then in the course of him being picked up for another murder or something else, his DNA would be checked, and a match would go against that found at Donna's murder. That can only happen, though, if the police allow for such matching. If the DNA results are secured in the sealed autopsy, then it isn't going to be much good.

There is too much interference, even to this day, by the San Diego Police Department to make one wonder if they are trying to hide something. It seemed like anytime Detective Streed got a sniff of something sketchy going on in the department, he was either shut out or sent away, as when he got taken off the task force. For an experienced detective, I think you can put a great deal of credibility to his hunches or gut feelings. After all, a good investigator hones his skills and gets better at what he "feels" as an investigation proceeds. Streed seemed pretty sure that cops were involved in Donna's death and the department was protecting them.

The unfortunate truth is that as time goes by, the trail to Donna's killer is colder than the North Pole. After more than 30 years, the actual killer might be dead. That doesn't negate that there are still individuals out there who know what went down when she was killed. The next chapter presents some of the possibilities proposed over the years. None of them seem quite right, and some have been totally discounted. However, it is worth reviewing them as somebody just might read this, and something will ring a bell that might reopen the case.

12

Did The Cops Kill Her?

Over 30 years have passed since the high-profile murder of my cousin Donna Gentile. Her autopsy results are still sealed. There have been no new leads. If you look at the facts that are known and see what had been happening to Donna in the last year of her life, it isn't such a mystery.

However, Donna's murder is now classified as a cold case, which refers to a tangible crime scene or scene of an accident that has yet to be solved. In most instances, a cold case will typically involve major felony crimes or violent behavior, such as rape or murder. A cold case is often an unsolved mystery of a death.

The strange part is that the San Diego Police Department and District Attorney's Office seem to want to keep it cold. As reported in the last chapter, when Channel 8 in San Diego requested that the San Diego County Medical Examiner release Donna's autopsy under the California Public Records

Act, the request was turned down. The denial came with an admission that Donna's death was not an active investigation and there were no leads. If the rationale was that releasing the information would jeopardize an ongoing investigation, then keeping the autopsy sealed would make some sense. As it is, DNA is solving other well-publicized cold cases as  this book is being completed. Lieutenant Ken Nelson admitted that cold case detectives are not investigating any leads on Donna, but if someone were to come forward, the police want to make sure they have the right person.

Sorry, but the San Diego Police Department smacks of cover-up and protecting their own. Remember that the San Diego Sheriff's Department started the initial investigation, since her body was dumped in the county, but the case was eventually transferred to the Metropolitan Homicide Task Force. The task force was charged with the investigation of not only Donna's murder but also others that were believed to be a series of prostitute murders.

An unfortunate aspect of law enforcement is that the police figure prostitutes are to blame for any mistreatment they encountered, including being murdered. They were treated as a non-person and often disregarded as legitimate victims of crime. If a prostitute reported that she was beaten, the cops wouldn't go out of their way to make any arrests. A prostitute's murder didn't receive as much attention as somebody else. The unspoken philosophy was that a prostitute or somebody like a drug dealer was already committing a crime, so they got what they deserved. It was the idea that

two wrongs make a right!

The Metropolitan Homicide Task Force's primary goal was not to solve Donna's or any other prostitute's murder but to salvage the public image of the San Diego Police Department. The police force was constantly in the newspapers facing various corruption charges and questionable practices. Donna's involvement with Black and Avrech was not the first case to reach the public's attention of cops being with prostitutes. There were others. The police department was in great need of rehabilitating a very tarnished reputation.

Often, Donna's murder was grouped in with any murder that had to do with a prostitute. One such case was Ronald Elliott Porter, a former Escondido auto mechanic who murdered a prostitute by the name of Sandra Cwik. Her body was found in 1989 in the same area where Donna

Murdered prostitute Sandra Cwik.

was discovered. Five women testified during a trial that Porter assaulted them. He would choke his victims to unconsciousness, and then rape them. He was also charged with the murders of Carol Jane Gushrowski and others. Donna's murder was tied to him for a while, but the evidence didn't match up.

There was also Cynthia Maine who was a friend of Donna's. She and Donna were the first two paid informants of Internal Affairs, and both were murdered. There was also talk of other murders linked to Donna, but hers was different than all of them. Her death was the only one that got two cops fired and brought reports of corrupt cops into the news. No matter how much the San Diego Police Department wanted to tie in other murders of prostitutes with Donna's killing, they were different.

Police Chief Bill Kolender 1975-1988

Captain Mike Tyler, who was the head of the Criminal Intelligence Unit of SDPD, worked on the Cynthia Maine murder along with other prostitute murders. Tyler owned Tyler's Feed in Alpine, which supplied hay and grain to the stable where Donna rode and stabled her horse Fantasia. Before Tyler retired from the Eastern Division, he ordered Sergeant Joe Cunningham and his officers not to cooperate with the Sheriff's Department investigating Donna's homicide.

During a grand jury in 1989-90, Chief Bill Kolender and Tyler were less than truthful and didn't have a good memory of anything. Chief Kolender had reinstated Black. You figure?

Over time, Donna's death was linked to people as varied as Gary Leon Ridgway, who was known as the Green River Killer, a convicted serial killer who lost count of how many women he murdered. The problem there was that he operated exclusively in the state of Washington. Then there was Glesty Waters, a man arrested in San Diego, who was mistaken for the Green River Killer. Glesty was arrested by Detectives Jeff Dean and John Lusardi, who were the heads of the task force. Dean was the officer who identified Donna's body. Glesty was in prison for over a year until the evidence manufactured against him was dismissed and he was let go. Ridgway was apprehended in 2001 based on DNA evidence.

To show the potential corruption in the San Diego Police Department, Glesty alleged that Internal Affairs used a known prostitute and intimidated her with prison threats if she didn't follow through on their fabricated story on Glesty. She was coerced to pick Glesty out in a lineup for the Green River Killer. This was all around the time of Donna's murder. She lives in hiding today.

  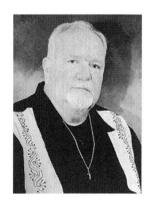

Left to right: Detective John Lusardi, Gary Leon Ridgway, and Glesty Waters.

To illustrate why a prostitute would be a victim of a serial killer, here is an excerpt from a letter by Dr. Annie Sprinkle, Founder of "Day To End Violence Against Sex Workers" when talking about Gary Ridgway, the Green River Killer:

Ridgway said, *"I picked prostitutes as victims because they were easy to pick up without being noticed. I knew they would not be reported*

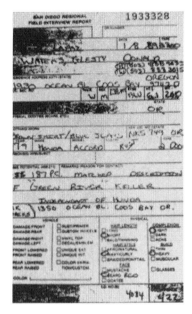

missing right away and might never be reported missing." He confessed to having murdered ninety women. Boyfriends and pimps were afraid to come forward with the fear of getting arrested. Ridgway's killing spree went on for over twenty years. Violent crimes against sex workers go unreported, unaddressed and unpunished. People don't care when prostitutes are victims of hate crimes, beaten, raped, and murdered. Regardless, they are part of neighborhoods, communities, and families.

Glesty Waters arrest ticket, "Wrongly Accused" author.

Then there was Karen Wilkening, the Rolodex Madam, who had associations with Lusardi and Donna. Wilkening was with Donna at a party three days before her murder. She was questioned but had no answers. Wilkening and Donna networked from time to time. Wilkening was a fugitive who fled to the Philippines from 1987 to 1989 and then returned to California to be arrested by Detective Lusardi. She alleges that she was friends with cops and detectives because she allegedly provided dancers for vice cops' bachelor parties.

Witness ties Gentile to Wilkening

She also ID's 12 cops as connected to jailed madam

This report was prepared by staff writers Jim Okerblom, Dayna Lynn Fried and J. Stryker Meyer

Another possible suspect in her murder was Steven

James. When homicide uncovered Donna's personal effects at her home, Steven's name was found in her "trick book." Steven was known to videotape prostitutes. He also had sadomasochistic fetishes which at times could be violent if the other person was agreeable.

Another murderer tied to Donna was Allen Michael (Buzzard) Stevens. Glesty Waters shared a cell with Buzzard for a number of months. Stevens killed Cynthia McVey in November 1988, one of the last of the prostitutes murdered that were under the Task Force investigation. Glesty alleges that Stevens bragged to him about belonging to a local secret organization that was killing snitching prostitutes. He described in detail how to snap someone's neck to paralyze them.

During their investigation, the police mainly pulled suspects from Donna's clients. Many were checked out, and some became persons of interest. It could have been because they hung around with Donna quite often, or they had some kink in their sexual appetites and might have had a tendency toward violence. However, alibis checked out, or physical evidence was absent that

ALAN BUZZARD STEVENS
Murder defendant

by Chief Deputy District Attorney Brian Michaels that Stevens also made what she considered a veiled threat against her.

"He said he worked with an organization that took care of snitches," Ferguson testified.

By Dave Hasemyer
Tribune Staff Writer

A fatigued and babbling Alan Michael Stevens reportedly told an acquaintance that he was having trouble finding places to dump bodies the day the nude corpse of a woman he has been charged with murdering was discovered.

"The girls, the girls. I'm running out of places to hide the bodies,'" was how Lori Ferguson recounted to a Superior Court jury yesterday part of a nearly incoherent conversation she had with Stevens.

Ferguson said she met Stevens two days before Cynthia McVey was found dead in North County. At the time Stevens made the remark about the bodies, Ferguson said, he had come to her house in Oceanside offering to help her and her husband move.

Recalling for Michaels the same encounter with Stevens, Ferguson said he told her how to kill a person.

"He showed me how you could put your hands just right on the back of somebody's neck and kill them," Ferguson said while holding her hands as if demonstrating a stranglehold.

would link any suspect to the murder.

Again, in today's world of sophisticated DNA testing, nothing has shown up. Anyone apprehended for a crime has to give a DNA sample along with their photo and fingerprints. DNA is run against data banks of DNA recovered from other crimes to see if there is a match. There is also other DNA information out there with which to compare samples. A serial killer from the 1970s in California was recently caught when a link was established between the man and DNA given by a relative for one of those ancestry tests. While this will be sure to open up a discussion of privacy on a person's DNA, the fact is that it was the key that allowed law enforcement to identify the killer after so much time.

My family has had a lot of time to reflect on Donna's murder. If the killer or killer is still alive out there, they need to be brought to justice. A beautiful young woman was brutally killed. She left home as a runaway and had to do whatever she could to survive. Donna certainly didn't want to live that life forever, and she had her entire adult life ahead of her. She could be enjoying grandchildren now if her life wasn't ended.

Who killed her? The police? You decide!

If you look at the evidence, the answer begins to appear obvious. The problem is that figuring out exactly which cop or cops did it is impossible. You need the San Diego Police Department, or better yet, an outside agency, to look at who was in the department 30 years ago in a completely unbiased manner.

Why do I say this? Let's look at a few key facts.

The crime scene did not give up many clues. The area around Donna's body was brushed free of tracks of any kind. Only a professional criminal or someone involved in law enforcement would know to take such precautions at a murder scene. Most criminals are caught because they aren't that bright and invariably leave some clues behind. If Donna's death was the result of a random John she met with for sex, the odds are very good that her body would not have been laid out so neatly. The same is true if it was a random murder.

On the subject of Donna being a victim of a serial murderer, other than being a prostitute and her body found in the general area where another murder victim would be found four years later, her death didn't meet the parameters of any known serial victims at the time. One of the things that tend to get serial murderers captured is that there are great similarities between their victims. In any of the known serial murders anywhere near San Diego at the time, Donna's death did not fit any profile.

The one big clue in Donna's murder was the gravel stuffed down her mouth. As the coroner's report showed, the gravel down her throat was the ultimate cause of her death. A dead person found like that is usually associated with being a snitch, and generally against the Mob. Donna had no known contacts with anyone in organized crime. While anything is possible, it does not seem plausible with the known information on Donna's activities and contacts that her death was Mob related. If there was, that is something the police would have jumped on in their investigation. If for no other reason than it would have taken attention off the police themselves as a potential suspect.

If Donna weren't a snitch for a criminal organization, then the obvious people that had to worry about her talking would have been the cops. Before we look at the possible culprits of the crime, let's look at another reason the San Diego Police Department cast guilt on themselves in the matter.

Remember that Thomas Streed, a veteran homicide investigator for the San Diego Sheriff's Department, was in charge of Donna's murder investigation at the beginning.

Whenever he tried to get information from the San Diego Police Department, he met with a "Blue Wall" of silence. He needed to meet a cop on the side to try and get any worthwhile information from the police. Even when he was on the Metropolitan Homicide Task Force, he was still trying to find a connection with Donna's murder to someone on the police force, and the cops repulsed him for his efforts. For an investigator with his experience, Streed must have had a good hunch of there being police involvement with Donna's death because of his concentration on that area of inquiry.

If the cops had something to do with Donna's death, there are two obvious candidates: Larry Avrech and Carl Black. As I have detailed in this book with what is known, the two were both involved with Donna. It wasn't a love triangle, but one of power. As a lieutenant, Black was the senior cop and took a great interest in Donna. While they were probably having sex together, Black tried to look after Donna and keep her out of trouble. He seemed to genuinely want to give Donna a chance to get out of the life she was in and get herself in a better position.

I believe that Avrech was envious and resented Black. Not for being with Donna, but for the position he held in the police department. Black had his Colorado River trip and had the respect of his peers. In the hierarchy of the San Diego Police Department, Black was the total insider. Avrech, on the other hand, was the outsider. He came across to others as a malcontent from the day he sued the city for not giving him what he thought he should have when he first became a full-time cop. That type of label is not something a person can easily shake in an organization like the police. Larry seemed to try hard to become more of an insider, and for that reason took on Black. Avrech resented that the lieutenant could get away with certain things and he could not.

This pulled Donna into the Civil Service hearing that was broadcast for all to see. It was there that Donna revealed to the public that she was a police informant. The result of the battle between Avrech and Black was that the department threw Avrech off the force and gave Black a temporary demotion. So who killed Donna?

Donna's body was discovered the day that Avrech was found guilty of the allegations brought against him and fired from the police department. It is logical that he had a motive against Donna and killed her for her testimony. He was easy fodder for the police to go after and he was a suspect for a while, but nothing tied him to Donna's death in any way. It seems perfectly possible that he was the catalyst to her death as he was the one who most likely orchestrated having TV cameras in the room during Donna's testimony against him and Black. It is entirely possible that for the first time, many cops found out that Donna was a police informant working for Internal Affairs to tell on dirty cops.

Larry Avrech's life went downhill for quite some time after being fired from the police force. He became the villain, was emotionally damaged, eventually lost his family, and was homeless for a time. Because of the investigation, the department alienated Avrech from friends associating with him, and people's jobs were later threatened if they were seen talking to him. Currently, he is also writing a book on Donna's death and his opinion of what happened to her and him. I have communicated and met with Larry. I do not think he killed my cousin, but I do feel his actions during his Civil Service hearing put a target on her back. Larry put Donna in the middle and used her as a prop to get back at the department.

Carl Black's hearing was to begin the day after Donna's body was found. That was June 25, 1985. After seeing the result of Avrech's hearing, he could have had a motive for killing Donna. He wouldn't want her testimony to screw up his career. It might seem like a good idea to eliminate her before the Civil Service Commission could ask her any more questions that might hurt his case. Black was helping Donna and she didn't know that by reporting Avrech, Black would go down. Her intentions were not to hurt Black in anyway. It just happened; it was out of her control. From what I understand, his daughter allegedly was bothered by this whole fiasco from the beginning. The demotion of her father, the murder of Donna, and the police corruption that she knew about caused her anxiety.

This possibility is not as easy to dismiss as Avrech killing Donna. While it might seem to go against Black's genuine fondness for Donna and wanting to help her, there is no telling what a person will do when backed into a corner. One of the problems with this scenario is that Donna spent hours on the stand that day during Larry Avrech's hearing, so how much more could she add against Black that wasn't already said? Unfortunately, that is a question we will never have an answer to.

Carl Black could have killed her or sent others to kill her to make sure that she didn't say anything else. Donna was pressured at this point to speak about her relationship with Black. If Avrech hadn't started harassing Donna and prying into her relations with Black none of this would of happened. Avrech's actions coerced Donna to take action against him, which in light brought Black into the triangle. The thing to remember about Avrech and Black is the actual hearing Donna appeared at was several months before her death. Soon after the hearing, Donna served her time in jail for the prostitution charges. She went in on the work-furlough program for three months that Black helped get her into for her stay. It is hard to say what could have changed in his mind to get rid of Donna after she came out of prison. Perhaps Avrech was framed?

We have to remember Donna's own words when she went to prison. On March 13, 1985, the day she entered jail, she made the tape that she left with her attorney that said:

Donna's tape-recorded words

"In case I disappear somewhere or am missing, I want my lawyer to give this to the press. I have no intention of disappearing or going out of town without letting my lawyer know first. Because of the publicity that I have given a police scandal, this is the reason why I'm making this. I feel someone in a uniform with a badge can still be a serious criminal. This is the only life insurance that I have."

The insurance didn't work.

Another source to back up this concept is an article in the Anchorage Daily News. Reporter Al Hajj Frederick Minshall wrote in January 2013:

"I worked at the San Diego County Mental Health facility, at the time adjacent to University of California Medical Center. San Diego Police Officers and County sheriffs frequently brought in "suspects" and prisoners for psychiatric evaluation. A few days after Ms. Gentile's murder, a black female Sheriff's Deputy assigned to Las Colinas brought a female prisoner to County Mental Health. The Deputy told me that Gentile had "...begged not to be released, because the cops were waiting for her."

"I published an article containing this information in the next edition of the "San Diego Voice & Viewpoint". Two or three days after its release the editor told me her paper could no longer accept copy from me, and she explicitly stated the police pressured her to fire me because of that article. It may have been Sun Tzu who said, "If your enemies attack you, it is a good thing—thus you know you are effective." Were Ms. Gentile still alive, she might argue that it's possible to have too much of a good thing in that regard."

"Not long after, and again while on duty at CMH, an SDPD officer warned me against antagonizing the commander of the department's Vice-Squad by continuing to publicly mention the Gentile and other prostitute murders that implicated cops, because "...that guy is a killer." I will not name this officer, or identify him beyond stating that he had testified at one of the Penn trials."

It seemed obvious that Donna felt pressure or threatened by cops. It could have been Avrech or Black in connection with the charges brought against them, but there are two other possibilities. One is that cops did it in retaliation for bringing one of their own, Lt. Carl Black, down. Causing trouble for an officer with his rank probably didn't sit well with many cops. There could have been a feeling that if she did this to him, who else could Donna or someone else cause trouble for on the force? Much like criminals do to "send a message," certain cops could have killed Donna and used the gravel in the mouth as a warning to others not to cause problems for the cops.

I have to think that Donna opened many different possibilities when it came out in the public hearing for Avrech that she was a police informant. That is not something you ever want to be broadcast like that. How many cops had to start wondering if Donna had something on them and was cooperating with Internal Affairs to bring them down? The revelation that this cute, well-spoken prostitute was an informer had to start a panic. The problem is that somebody on the force could be so paranoid about what they were doing wrong that they could think Donna was informing on them even if it was not a case.

Whoever did it used the gravel in the mouth to let the world know that Donna was a snitch, and this is what happened to snitches. It is certainly plausible that Donna could have been picked up, done some cocaine with someone (she had it in her system), had sex (semen found in her), and then was killed. It is a horrible way to end such a young life, but her fear of being killed by the police adds extra significance to it happening at the hand of one or more cops.

The San Diego Police Department was very corrupt at the time Donna lived in the city. It is scary that motives and techniques usually attributed to organized crime are so easily talked about as ways the police operate. For as long as there have been police, many forces operate on their own underground rules to keep order in the department. Sometimes this means corruption on a huge scale as payoffs from criminals is a way of doing business. It can mean that the prostitutes of a city are treated as the private brothel of the force. Whatever the corruption, it is not unknown for the police to take matters into their own hands to safeguard what they have.

With the time that has gone by, finding who was responsible for Donna's death might never be known. If there is anything helpful in her autopsy, it is only known by the police who are keeping it sealed.

Nobody deserves to die as Donna did. Every life is precious whether you are the head of a country, the CEO of big business, a working mother with kids, or a prostitute trying to make a living. I hope that anybody reading this who might have some clue of what happened to Donna, even after all this time, would make an effort to contact me or the authorities. She was a good person, she would have grown up, and I believe she would have had a stable, normal life with children. In a world where hate is prominent one can only get tired of saving themselves. We could only harness her spirit and feel her presence.

We Live and Learn or Die and others Learn...Learned Lessons come in all forms...

TAPE: Prostitute Feared Retaliation

Continued from Page 4

conduct with a prostitute after Gentile said she had sex with Avreck in exchange for favors. Gentile denied having sex with Black.

Neither Avreck nor Black could be reached for comment Friday.

City records show that Gentile also filed an administrative claim against the city this year in which she alleged that she was continually harassed by several San Diego officers. The claim said she had received numerous traffic citations during a Police Department sweep of prostitutes on El Cajon Boulevard. She was cited for throwing a cigarette on a sidewalk, parking more than 18 inches from a curb and failing to have a working defroster in her car.

Gentile left jail May 5 and moved

brook, said Friday that she gave him the tape as she was being taken into jail March 13, telling him to give the tape to Bob Donley, a reporter for KGTV (Channel 10).

KGTV played part of the recording on the air Friday night. Donley said the tape was turned over to Sheriff's Department homicide detectives investigating Gentile's death.

United Press International on Friday quoted Sheriff's Lt. Bill Baxter as saying Avreck and Black had been contacted by homicide detectives investigating the Gentile case.

"I wouldn't go as far as to consider them suspects at this point," Baxter told UPI.

Holbrook said Friday that Gentile had told him many times in the past several months that she feared Avreck. He said Gentile did not

the circumstances surrounding the slaying to satisfy his own curiosity.

"Certainly, I have a personal interest in wanting to find out who did something to one of my clients," Holbrook said. "I have not been retained for that purpose. The concern I have is that since police were involved, I'm not sure what their inclination is to investigate it."

Police spokesman Bill Robinson said the department is not investigating any connection Avreck might have to Gentile's death. He said the department's role in the case ended when Avreck was fired.

Louis Gentile said Friday that he could not afford to hire an attorney or private detective to investigate his sister's death.

"Right now all I can do is sit and wait," he said.

Slain woman linked to police sex case

By Vicki Torres
Tribune Staff Writer

A woman found 11 days ago beaten and strangled near Juniper Highway in Pine Valley has been identified as Donna Marie Gentile, a convicted prostitute whose involvement with two San Diego police officers resulted in the sentence of one and the firing of another.

Coroner David Stark said the body was dragged through fingerprints at the time grandstand arrests of Gentile, 22, at the 4700 block of Club Street in Normal Heights.

The body was discovered at 8 p.m. June 23.

Deputy Sheriff Dan Jackson has ___ north of ___ Interstate 8 and two miles west of Sunrise Highway near a turnoff road, Stark said.

The body had a disheveled dress, shoes and undergarments and had both bruises and marks on the neck, Stark said. Investigators said she had been bruised and strangled.

Death must have occurred a short time before the body was found, Stark said, because the body showed no signs of decomposition.

Further tests were planned for the presence of drugs or poison and to determine whether Gentile was sexually molested before her death, Stark said.

Gentile's landlord contacted the coroner's office Monday to report her missing, and a check of fingerprints was made, Stark said.

Sheriff's homicide detectives investigating Gentile's death urged anyone with possible information on the case to contact the Sheriff's Department.

Police authorities have confirmed two police are on the grounds that they had carried on inappropriate relationships with Gentile from June 1984 to September.

Please see BODY, B-2

Police confirm 2 officers' relationship with prostitute

By Terry L. Colvin
Staff Writer

A San Diego police patrolman who has been fired and a lieutenant who has been recommended for dismissal

violations of the law — could not be substantiated well enough to bring criminal charges.

"But that doesn't mean we don't ___

and that I shouldn't go to jail," Amos did not reduce the woman's sentence.

"I did receive a letter from a policeman at the time of sentencing."

13

A Voice For All Women

Along with all the collected news articles and family stories that I carried around with me for years, and my fact-findings, I came across Cal State Professor Jerry Kathleen Limberg's 2012 YouTube presentation, "The Murder of Donna Gentile: San Diego Policing and Prostitution 1980-1993." She was responsible for putting together the first comprehensive narrative concerning Donna's death. One of the original concepts for her research was to discuss the historical relationships between police and prostitutes dating back to the 19th century.

Her quest brought her into contact with a book titled "NHI," which was put together by a group of San Diego artists in 1992. The book was a gathering of information about those forty-three women killed in the '80s in the San Diego area. The book was a result of the artists' outrage that law enforcement didn't work very hard on those deaths because the women lived on the outskirts of society. The authors were appalled at law enforcement's use of the term "NHI," which was an acronym for "No Humans Involved," and for the word annihilation. The term was used by cops to depict victims that weren't worth their time because they were "unworthy" of justice or protection because of their crimes. Limberg's subsequent work on her research compiled, organized, and helped shed a timeline on the events leading up to Donna's death as depicted in this book. NHI was an old police term that goes back in murder history on the East Coast. Its purpose was to act as a wake-up call against ongoing naked male aggression, a reminder that warped habits die hard and that female victims continue to be blamed for the violence perpetrated against them.

NHI Gallery Installation

Credit: Deborah Small, Scott Kessler, Elizabeth Sisco, Carla Kirkwood, & Louis Hock

Her original finding of "NHI" illustrates how prostitutes were looked at by cops and other people. Prostitutes are looked down upon by society. Often, they are treated as non-people. Generally, prostitutes do not want to do what they do; it is a way to survive. The hypocrisy that often revolves around the commercial sex trade, especially in America, is immense. You have cops, government officials, and judges fighting it, but very often those cops, government officials, and judges are active participants. All you have to do is look at the recent "Me Too" movement to see how many people who advocate for justice for women are forced to resign when their secrets see the light of day. I believe that if you take the biblical concept of *"He who is without sin should throw the first stone,"* then there wouldn't be too many men out there paying lip service to how bad prostitution is.

NHI Gallery Installation

Credit: Deborah Small, Scott Kessler, Elizabeth Sisco, Carla Kirkwood, & Louis Hock

In death, her voice is one of the many that speaks for all of the prostitutes as if to say, *"We are people. We are women. We count as much as anyone else."*

A voice is all anyone has. This is especially true for

women, who bring life into the world. The voice of women today is both courageous and alive. It took great efforts, including the women's rights movement, to bring the voices of women to a greater volume in the present time. If Donna's predicament had happened today, she might still be alive. My cousin Donna was a courageous, strong woman who carved a path and stood up for her rights in the 1980s. Strong women then and now can be intimidating and cause confusion and fear. People wonder where they get their strength and where they are going with it, like Diana, Princess of Wales once said. The SDPD had this fear of a strong woman that was too close for comfort. That was still a time when even female politicians weren't as visible as they are today. She was a member of the so-called "oldest profession" who was victimized by authority and fought back by speaking out. As a result, she lost her life, but her actions and her sacrifice lent focus to the maxim on women's equality:

"When one suffers, we all suffer." Anita

NHI Gallery Installation

Credit: Deborah Small, Scott Kessler, Elizabeth Sisco, Carla Kirkwood, & Louis Hock

NHI Gallery Installation

Credit: Deborah Small, Scott Kessler, Elizabeth Sisco, Carla Kirkwood, & Louis Hock

As I have said before, although Donna found herself working as a street prostitute, it wasn't something she chose. Survivorship decided her calling. In an evolving world, prostitution has come a long way, with prostitutes now often called *sex workers* and available on the internet and with regular advertising. This term was coined by sex worker activist Carol Leigh in 1978. She believed that the laws against sex workers are a form of discrimination and that finding a resource against violence should be the goal of the fight to legalize or decriminalize the profession. It is clear that poverty and violence lead to the most abject forms of prostitution. Sex work itself has moved to a different arena.

On sober reflection, the city street is where many things begin. It is an arena where protests occur and where people march for their rights as part of movements such as "Black Lives Matter." It is where the homeless live, where drug trade and sex trade is common. Yet, it is also where holiday parades glimmer, where races are run, and where children play.

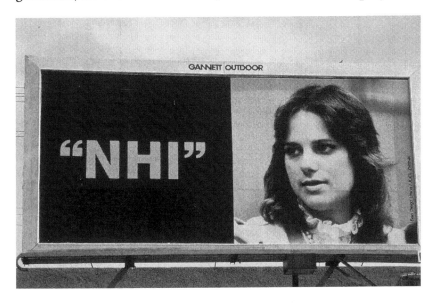

Donna NHI billboard photo faced the SDPD.

Credit: Deborah Small, Scott Kessler, Elizabeth Sisco, Carla Kirkwood, & Louis Hock

Women in all walks of life are vulnerable. They seek love, protection, support, and security. Those who work in the sex industry are no exception. Admittedly, they are stigmatized because they are engaging in illegal activity, but they are part of the fabric of society providing a service. It has always been so. You can find prostitution talked about in the earliest books of the Old Testament in the Bible. The ancient Greek and Roman civilizations had palaces for prostitution. Sex has always been a prominent service industry. Let's face it; if there weren't a real demand for such service, the profession couldn't be sustained. All in all, a woman is a person regardless of her work, and her voice deserves attention and reflection.

This book has been about an all-too-human woman who found herself a prostitute at the start of her early life journey. Donna was someone who, if given the opportunities others had, would have prevailed. To bring this story to a conclusion, I must educate you a little about prostitution, giving you some insight as to what it is, where it began, and who gets into it, to deepen your appreciation on the topic.

Prostitution began as far back as in the primal days when chimpanzees (bonobos) used sex not just to reproduce but for recreation as well. They also would practice sexual activities as a greeting and to resolve conflicts with sex instead of aggression. Female chimpanzees had to give sex to male chimpanzees to get the bananas from the tree. Bonobo is one of the closest relatives to humans along with the chimpanzee. They live in the Democratic Republic of Congo in central Africa. These simian creatures endure colorful sex lives; unlike other simians, the bonobo female genitalia is tilted forward much like that of a human female. Because of this, they can practice face to face sex with a variety of positions like humans do. Bonobos by habit engage in sex once a day but frequently several times per day. They engage in oral sex, group sex, and even deep kissing. They even have the ability to gaze into each other's eyes during sex in ways that are impossible for other mammals. Bonobos resemble human structure physically more closely than any other primate. They are the closest human relative in the animal kingdom.

A prostitute, also known as a sex worker, is a person who trades sexual behavior in some form for money or other negotiable assets. Sex work may be used to refer to those in all areas of the sex industry including not only those who provide the sexual services but also the staff of the industry. The term sex work became popularized after the publication of an anthology compiled by women in the sex industry in 1987. This term is still considered controversial by social conservatives, anti-prostitution feminists, and other prohibitionists.

On another note, prostitution is like rape over and over again, and that is one reason why it's evolved as a healing method for both worker and client. Sex workers and clients harmonize in the sessions, and the sex worker has more control of her body and emotions. The session becomes a spiritual, compassionate healing practice that is fulfilling for both. The reality is that sexual healing is necessary, like hunger and thirst. These are basic needs. Once we learn how to have a deeper understanding of love and respect toward all humans, then people can have healthier relationships.

Sex work and general sexual habits of anyone has increased since the "sexual revolution" movement made sex more open and free for all. This also became known as "sexual liberation." Dr. Wilhelm Reich, a medical doctor of the 1950s, coined the term "sexual revolution" and authored the book, "The Function of the Orgasm." He writes that sexuality is the center around which revolves the whole social life and the inner life of the individual.

There is a lot of shame and hiding around the area of sexuality. Men feel entitled to seek and act out on their desires more openly these days. Shame exists because of emotional wounds in both men and women of all orientations. When shame is present, there is always the chance of violence in sexuality. The goal is to prevent violence and provide a place where healing begins. Modern revolutions propelled the gay rights movement, feminism, and helped contribute to redefining women's sexuality.

Women find themselves in the sex work field often as a mere means of survival in the beginning, but as time goes on, it becomes a true profession for some. In the beginning, lack of education, skills, or single parenthood often leads to sex work out of desperation. Women in this business who survive may become resilient and desensitized emotionally because of the demand upon them and the pressure it places upon one's emotions. They also may end up dabbling in drugs because of the emotional strain the work demands of them.

From another angle, sex work may be considered a form of feminine freedom, a way to parade the body image and to seek glamour or attention. After all, men do obsess about the female body and women do go to great lengths to make their appearance pleasing to men. Sex work can be empowering to some, making a woman feel sexy and permitting her to live out her fantasies. *Feminism is a right to act any way you choose,* and this is no exception.

Women who choose sex work are comfortable with their sexuality. Women in all walks of life these days want to achieve sexual freedom and feel comfortable and empowered by their sexuality. There is more sexual integrity, freedom, and liberation these days. It is part of the time we live in today. Sex workers face shame and discrimination from peers, but the work also makes them feel welcomed and accepted, and gives them that permission to be who they want to be. Sex workers today have more autonomy and more personal liberty to embark on this path.

Once upon a time, the only women who would dress provocatively were those who were selling their bodies. Today women and girls dress to attract sexual attention and bare parts they would never have in the past. Often the everyday woman can be easily mistaken for a prostitute. The objectification of women has evolved, generations have changed, and the stigma is moving forward. If there is judgment toward a sex worker, it should also be there for the consumer; after all, it takes two to tango.

The age-old problem with prostitution is that it has been looked down on as being immoral. Thus, laws are constructed against it, and law enforcement must enforce those laws. It makes cops and prostitutes traditional enemies. The irony here is that the prostitutes often engage in sexual harassment from the cops. It is bad enough that the prostitutes have to be worried about being hauled to jail by the police, but they often find themselves having to service the cops.

Donna's story was not atypical concerning her relationship with the cops. If a police officer found a well-spoken, clean, young woman like Donna, he was going to target her for more than an arrest. He was going to be attracted to someone like that, and if she would do a few favors for him (sex), he could do some for her up to a certain point. Just as prostitution for money is a business transaction, so was doing favors to avoid trouble. It was a form of commerce that seemed to operate at a high level in the San Diego Police Department but wasn't that different from any other major city.

The cops would fuck a girl, but that didn't mean they held her in high regard. It is abominable behavior because, while the cops would happily use these girls, to them, prostitutes were part of the underclass and were considered expendable and classified as NHI. No matter what and who you are, all lives do matter! There is someone who loves that person who might have been beaten or killed. Police are supposed to serve and protect no matter who you are. Being a prostitute is one thing but being sexually harassed by a police officer is another. Donna looked to police for protection like any other citizen. Not only was it denied her; it killed her. No one should be a criminal and a victim.

The "NHI" — No Humans Involved — movement resulted from activists coming together to show the power of women and to expose the truth of how "marginal" people are treated. The project was unveiled on February 19, 1992, with two billboards that faced both the county administration center and the San Diego Police headquarters, bearing the picture of Donna and the logo "NHI." The goal of the NHI project was to pay tribute to the murdered women, raise public awareness about the series of murders and the botched police investigation, and relate the local reaction to the crimes to larger social attitudes toward general violence. The purpose of NHI was to humanize the victims and demonstrate that violence against any woman is unacceptable.

The collaborative project was designed by Deborah Small, Scott Kessler, Elizabeth Sisco, Carla Kirkwood, and Louis Hock.

"I'm in there! I'm one of the Women in that Picture!"

Margot Leigh Butler

The NHI established an exhibition of public art projects about community issues that addressed the sexual assault and murder of the 45 San Diego women between 1985 and 1992. The storefront gallery exhibition in downtown San Diego gave a face to the 45 murdered women. The project invited women to donate their photos to the exhibition in honor of these women. Dick Lewis headed up the San Diego Metropolitan Homicide Task Force that was investigating the women's murders and the connected police corruption. He publicly stated that he chose to withhold the murdered women's photographs from the NHI project. Lewis played both sides of the fence and hypocritically later told the San Diego Tribune that "transients and their families were probably glad they were gone." They lumped these girls photos together as if their lives didn't matter: *"people are a person with feelings."*

Many women came forward and donated images in place of the slain women, including former LAPD officer Norma Jean Almodovar, who is also the author of "Cop to Call Girl" and founder of ISWFACE. Donna's attorney, Douglas Holbrook, also attended. One of the women, Megan, called out,

"I'm one of the girls in that picture!" Megan's exclamation articulated a way of acknowledging that all women are a part of a relational, collective, and powerful whole. The most moving part of "NHI" was MWI or "Many Women Involved," the performance component of NHI created by Carla Kirkwood. I had the opportunity of seeing this back in 1993 at Highways Performance Space and Gallery in Los Angeles and that is where I saw Donna's face in this installation for the first time. Carla Kirkwood's spoken word concluded that "we are all part of one another" and what happens to one happens to all.

The project included public presentations, videotapes, newspapers, and information booklets. The commitment involved Parrhesia, which means freedom of speech. Donna was parrhesiastes where she spoke in the face of danger. It is a courage to speak the truth at risk. Sometimes not to speak is to lie; silence can at times be a form of violence. In turn, her spoken voice caused violence. *"Her parrhesiastic mouth was stuffed." From the book Killing Women. Margot Leigh Butler. (book edited by Annette Burfoot and Susan Lord)*

"There is no greater agony than bearing an untold story inside you."

Maya Angelou

A recent movie titled "Three Billboards Outside Ebbing, Missouri" starring Frances McDormand is a film about a billboard calling out cops. It portrayed a lack of justice that real life women often face. American writer Allan G. Johnson calls it "Misogyny, a cultural attitude of hatred for females," but American academic Camille Paglia would argue it is a fear of females.

It is important to note that the media coverage for the NHI project perpetuated the myth that the slain women were first and foremost prostitutes, drug addicts, and transients. Public perception of the murders was framed by this generalized idea labeling all the victims as "bad girls." One of the NHI collaborators, Elizabeth Sisco, added, "Hopefully, the light was shed on the danger faced by all women in a society that denies the true culprits in the 'wages of sin' favoring the comfort of the false dichotomy created by the good girl/bad girl label." The good girl is a familiar archetype for many women in that it can overpower her with limitation.

Often victims are blamed for violence perpetrated against them. Police labeled these women as throwaway women that existed on the fringe of society and because of that, there was a lack of justice. Law enforcement demonstrated negative attitudes towards these women and didn't put any effort into solving their murders. If a prostitute was raped, law enforcement viewed it as something that went with the job. It was this abuse that a victim of prostitution had to deal with when it came to the law.

The effort I talk about here concerning the NHI movement occurred in the 1990s. While they brought awareness to the problem of prostitutes and sex workers being treated as something less than people, the problem is ongoing today. In a February 2018 article in "Time" magazine, Samantha Cooney wrote an article titled, "They Don't Want to Include Women Like Me. Sex Workers Say They're Being Left Out of the #MeToo Movement." The article talks to current and former sex workers about how they are still pushed out on the fringes of society. Somebody in business or Hollywood can talk about sexual abuse and harassment, and anger and public opinion will come down on the perpetrator like a ton of bricks. However, with a sex worker, the attitude still is, "Look at the work you do. What did you expect?"

Donna's involvement with police and her subsequent death occurred 35 years ago. To some, that might seem like ancient history. A revealing paragraph from Cooney's article states:

"A 2014 report submitted to the United Nations by three sex worker advocacy organizations documented a pattern of abuse by police towards sex workers that includes "assault, sexual harassment, public 'gender searches' (police strip searches for the purpose of viewing genitalia) and rape." A 2016 Department of Justice report, launched after the April 2015 police custody death of Freddie Gray, found indications that the Baltimore Police Department disregarded reports of sexual assault from people in the sex industry, and some officers targeted people in the sex industry "to coerce sexual favors from them in exchange for avoiding arrest, or for cash or narcotics."

What Donna experienced is still going on, and prostitutes and other sex workers are still looked at as people who do not deserve the same protections as everybody else in the eyes of the law.

Sex workers today lead a movement to legalize their work because, in some cases, it has evolved to the level of educated therapeutic healing. Sex work is an up-and-coming career choice for both men and women these days who may have furthered their education with doctorates in sex therapy, tantra, somatic sex, sexology, sex surrogacy, and more. Such a sex worker views sex from a healing standpoint in that sex is a basic human need, and without the opportunity there to fulfill this need, violence in the world may increase. While there is much controversy around this subject, certain places have legalized it. These include parts of the state of Nevada, the city of Amsterdam, Australia, and some locations in Canada and Israel. The future of the movement is at stake, given that sex wars exist between the feminist sex workers' rights movement and the feminist abolitionists. Feminists and sex workers must find common ground and come together as sisters to strengthen the bonds of women seeking their rights.

In some places, common sense seems to be showing signs of life. San Francisco is a prime example. They began a policy that barred sex workers who reported, experienced, or witnessed violence from being arrested. In 1999, the St. James Infirmary opened; it is a health and safety clinic for sex workers. It was formed collaboratively through a team effort of sex workers and Coyote founder Margo St. James. It has a "Bad Date" app where sex workers can anonymously log and look up clients who have threatened, robbed, extorted, or been violent toward other sex workers in the past. This app may have been shut down with the new laws.

Movements like "Me Too" are not going to mean anything until they include all women. While there is an International Day to End Violence Against Sex Workers every December 17, it is going to take more than that. It is going to take the voice of someone like Donna Gentile to speak from beyond the grave to show women that any future progress to strengthen the rights of women can only happen when all women are included. It is the only way to save other women from suffering the same sad fate as Donna.

"I was born powerless as I died powerless"

I Came To This World

*"I came to this world riding a horse named love, every night is bright
with ecstasy and delight, since in my religion the intoxication by pure
wine is allowed you will never see my lips gone dried.*

RUMI

Thank you for hearing my voice... Donna Gentile

Epilogue

Donna is dead. Perhaps if we knew who killed her, she might be able to rest in peace. I am haunted by her spirit to bring this forth in her memory. It's been 33 years since the murder of Donna Gentile. Her case is unsolved, cold, and a mystery. Donna's murder is still a news topic as of today. Her autopsy is sealed forever. The San Diego community still wants answers. We the family believe that the autopsy should be made public. Donna is still alive in many hearts in the San Diego community.

Donna would be 55 years of age today in 2018. Donna's brother Louis is alive and living in Philadelphia, divorced from wife Pam. They had a son Anthony. Donna's mother, Ellen, and stepdad are alive and in their 70s. Roseann Gentile DeFrancesco, my mom and legal guardian to Lou Jr., passed away in 2007. Uncle Frank DeVincenzo, who brought Donna's body back from San Diego, has passed away also. The Tabor Children's Services Home in Doylestown, Penn. is still around and thriving.

Professor Jerry Limberg is a professor at California State University. Bonnie Dumanis, the District Attorney of San Diego, retired. She held office from 2003 to 2017. Her successor was DA Summer Stephan.

As far as the San Diego Police Department goes, it is there and functioning to serve and protect the community.

This primary law enforcement agency was established back in 1889. It is a much-improved department since the '80s, with lots of new players. Many changes and new developments and policies have been put into place.

El Cajon Boulevard is still there, but you won't see as many prostitutes these days since the sex-trafficking task force is in place. The internet also played a part in its reduction as a place to find prostitutes. Prostitution charges have increased to a sex traffic charge, which is a felony and a higher offense for a first-timer. As we know, prostitution is quite different than sex trafficking. Sex trafficking is much more of a crime as it involves pimps, mostly males who take underage children as hostage and pander them for sex. I am not sure why these two are lumped together. Senator Marty Block is pushing a bill that would increase the fines for men who buy sex, and the money would go toward rehabilitation for victims.

Sex for money has become challenging for the average sex worker offering consenting services with a client. SESTA/FOSTA has taken rights away from advertising on popular networking sites such as Craigslist and Backpage.

On February 27, 2018, the House of Representatives passed a bill that combined SESTA/FOSTA to stop enabling the sex traffickers. FOSTA allows states and victims to fight online sex trafficking. Many platforms are feeling threatened by this since even local businesses such as hotels can be fined if sex work goes on there and they are not aware.

Donna's case continues to be investigated. On June 28, 1990, Police Chief Bob Burgreen assigned assistant Chief Norm Stamper to review Donna's murder, which was being investigated with 40 other murder killings by the joint city-county Metropolitan Homicide Task Force. Donna's case has been investigated by so many different teams of detectives; it's puzzling why so many investigations continue. An answer is coming!

As for the players involved, some have passed away. Lt. Carl Black was later reinstated in 1986, from Sergeant back to Lieutenant, and he worked the SDPD until retirement. Black is in his 70s and living in Temecula, Calif. Larry Avrech is 66 and lives in Tennessee with his present wife, Nancy. After he was fired from the SDPD, he worked as a private investigator until retirement.

Lt. Larry Linstrom, whom Donna reported on occasion during her informant days, died on July 6, 2016. Sergeant Harold Goudarzi left the department because of an alleged intimate relationship with an informant prostitute and now works as a private investigator. Glesty Waters, the "Wrongly Accused" author, lives with his wife and sons in Oregon. Detective John Lusardi retired from the SDPD and works as a private investigator in Idaho. Karen Wilkening, the Rolodex Madam, is 71 and living in San Diego. Detective Jeff Dean recently retired after 29 successful years with the SDPD. He commanded the San Diego Police Department's Criminal Intelligence Unit. As of 2018, he is an investigator at San Diego Unified School District. Jeff Dean was the one who identified Donna's body at the murder scene and was also the arresting officer for Glesty Waters. Jeff was also one of the officers Donna reported on in her corruption claim.

Detective Thomas Streed has since then retired from the San Diego Sheriff's Department and lives in San Diego. He was one of the only detectives back then to hold a PhD degree. Officer Bob Candland retired and is also a private investigator. Detective Dick Lewis died of leukemia in 2010. Chief of Police Bill Kolender died Oct. 6, 2015 of Alzheimer's at age 80. He reformed the San Diego Police Department as chief from 1975 to 1988 and later became San Diego County Sheriff. Sgt. Norman Hardman died Aug.18, 2016. Detective Bob Hannibal lives in Vista, Calf. and now works as a traveling auto parts salesman. Captain Michael Tyler of Alpine Feed died in May 1995 of cancer. Chief of Police Norm Stamper retired living in Washington and has authored "Breaking Rank." SDPD Bob Burgreen passed in December 2007.

Attorney Douglas Holbrook was sincerely saddened by the death of his client Donna who was also a friend. He was very hurt and heartbroken as he worked diligently to help her case. He genuinely liked her and saw her potential to make a better life. He has since then passed on and is survived by his daughter Erica.

Michele Tennies, Donna's best friend, may still live in San Diego.

Over the years, several detectives took on the case and interviewed many people and gathered numerous report documents. Even new DNA testing was applied in 2007, which failed to identify anybody new. CC Moore of DNA Detectives has advanced knowledge in this area of work. The department has exhausted their leads, but those following this case are still waiting, hoping, and wanting an answer. As recently as 2015, CBS News 8 in San Diego interviewed Lt. Ken Nielson, and he felt there was no good reason for a sealed autopsy.

California State University Professor Jerry Limberg quotes: *"It shouldn't matter what happened. It matters that she was a human being."*

As far as serial killers, Allen Michael Buzzard Stevens died in his cell; Ronald Elliott Porter and Gary Ridgway, the Green River Killer, are serving life sentences.

As for the divine horse Fantasia, she went to live on with Donna's spirit somewhere over the rainbow. And as for all the people out there and everyone involved, we are all still learning and learning.

Afterword

Larry Avrech lives in Tennessee with his wife. After the scandal at the SDPD, he went on to work as a private investigator until retirement. He and his wife share the joy and love of their dachshunds. He stays mentally light in caring and loving these animals; he also has a unique comic book collection. He has two grown children whom he is very close to. We had the opportunity of meeting in 2017 in Philadelphia; we shared notes and feelings. I found him to be a sensitive human being, moving past his pain but still holding onto regret and sorrow. We shared good food, laughs, and interesting conversations.

Glesty Waters, the author of "Wrongly Accused," lives in Oregon with his wife and sons. He works in the auto business. He called me, along with his PI, Mike Kiger, on several occasions to discuss notes about Donna, with hopes of him getting his name cleared. He met with Donna's attorney, Douglas Holbrook, who re-opened his case. He shared videos, notes, and documents with me. We shared laughs and feelings.

About The Author

"The Donna Gentile Story" is the author's first publication within the genre of true crime. It is a true story, a story of tragedy, the story of a first cousin, a young woman, loving and kind, but silenced, abandoned when she speaks of her hardships at home, from there to prostitution, exploitation and death, a murder never resolved.

But Anita DeFrancesco has also written her own true story. She is the author of "Live Free — Re-create And Liberate Your Life," her own journey, a return from devastation, a return from the brutality of a sexual assault.

Anita lives, writes, and speaks as a woman who has not only survived her own challenges, but has also grown from it and re-created her life journey. She has used her painful and tragic experience to help other women and girls. Her extensive service includes UCLA/The Rape Foundation, Santa Monica College, Widener University, The Boys and Girls Club, Amity Foundation, Amistad de Los Angeles, The Clare Foundation, Share, DiDi Hirsch, and many others including LA's "Children of the Night," founded by Dr. Lois Lee, an organization that rescues child prostitutes from pimps and organized child sex traffickers. Early on Anita created a drug free group for teenagers called RAP. A two-time nationwide award winning journalist, she has been a columnist for Century City News in Los Angeles. She produced her own cable television and radio shows.

Currently living in Philadelphia, Penn., Anita is author, teacher, actress, therapist, and world traveler. She holds a Master of Arts degree in Psychology and is an active member of SAG/AFTRA. She teaches Yoga and is founder of Tantra Wisdom, offering regular classes on bonded relationships based on love, connection, and spirituality.

She can be found:

www.anitadefrancesco.com

Email: info@anitadefrancesco.com

Acknowledgments

I thank and acknowledge Professor Jerry Limberg of San Diego State University for her YouTube presentation she prepared on Donna and San Diego policing and prostitution. I'd also like to thank the media and news sources including the Bucks County Courier Times, The New York Times, The Los Angeles Times, The San Diego Union Tribune, Investigative Producer David Gotfredson of CBS news 8 KFMB, San Diego Voice & Viewpoint, San Diego Press, San Diego Reader, and the many other news sources that contributed to her ongoing story. I give thanks to the San Diego team of detectives for their efforts in trying to solve this case. I give special thanks to Detective Thomas Streed of the Homicide Division of the Sheriff's Department in San Diego for his comprehensive and detailed efforts on this case.

I acknowledge and thank family and mostly my mother, Roseanne Gentile DeFrancesco, for being a big part of this experience, and Donna's brother Lou who endured much pain and sorrow.

I acknowledge and thank Norma Jean Almodovar for her commitment on the subject of policing and prostitution. She is the founder of the International Sex Worker Foundation for Art, Culture, and Education in Los Angeles (ISWFACE). She serves as executive director for the Los Angeles branch of COYOTE.

I thank Melanie Dante for her passion, organization, and dedication on the annual "International Day To End Violence Against Sex Workers" every December 17 in Philly. It's been going on in Philadelphia at Thomas Paine Plaza outside of City Hall for about three years now, though SWOP, SAFE, and William Way have been holding Philly memorials since 2012.

I give thanks to Dr. Annie Sprinkle, who led the "Day to End Violence Against Sex Workers" memorial along with the Sex Workers Outreach Project, USA, starting in 2003 at the sentencing of Green River Killer, Gary Ridgway.

I give thanks to the NHI artists for their collaboration in bringing awareness and their permission for use of the photos. Deborah Small, Scott Kessler, Elizabeth Sisco, Carla Kirkwood, and Louis Hock.

I thank Larry Avrech for meeting with me and sharing his story and documents. I thank Glesty Waters and Mike Kiger for their support and sharing information and documents.

I thank others who supported and helped along the way: Carol Seelaus and Chadd Paul Davidson, M.D, for their writing support, Mary O'Connor for her voice, John Oliver Mason for believing, Cousin Regina Poolos, Chris Mangold and Gene Dillman for spirit. I thank Joe Cianfrani Sr. for his unconditional love, kindness, and foreverness.

I thank Dr. Timaree Leigh Schmit for bringing awareness; she can be found at https://sexwithtimaree.com/. I further thank Peter Zales of Affordable Offset Printing, JPac Productions for videography and website services, Nathan Kuruna for multimedia services, Johnny "Lemuria" Robinson for multimedia services, and Chris McDonough for technical services.

I'd like to thank JJ McKeever for his editing and writing support. He can be found at www.jjwriting-consulting.com.

I thank Di Freeze for her media and graphic talents. She can be found at www.freezetimemedia.com.

I thank Jonathan Borowko for cover illustration art. He can be found at https://www.linkedin.com/in/jonathan-borowko/.

Sources

- www.TheDonnaGentileStory.com

- http://articles.latimes.com/1985-07-06/local/
  me-9506_1_donna-gentile

- https://www.sandiegoreader.com/news/1988/sep/22/
  cover-bob-hannibal-was-one-of-the-good-guys-or-so/

- CBS-KFMB San Diego: http://www.cbs8.com/
  story/31344613/autopsy-remains-sealed-in-1985-
  murder-of-donna-gentile

- http://articles.latimes.com/1990-12-06/local/
  me-7896_1_task-force

- https://www.nbcsandiego.com/news/local/I-Was-Just-a-
  Man-Who-Wanted-Sex-Detective.html

- https://www.adn.com/voices/article/
  where-was-stand-your-ground-law-when-sagon-penn-
  needed-it-part-4/2013/01/17/

- https://www.adn.com/voices/article/
  where-was-stand-your-ground-law-when-sagon-penn-
  needed-it-part-3/2013/01/06/

- https://en.wikipedia.org/wiki/Choke-out

- http://articles.latimes.com/1991-07-27/local/me-49_1_
  police-officers

- http://articles.latimes.com/1991-05-16/local/me-2451_1_
  task-force

- http://articles.latimes.com/1991-07-31/local/me-107_1_
  san-diego-police

- http://articles.latimes.com/1991-05-17/local/me-1919_1_

san-diego

- http://articles.latimes.com/1990-09-27/local/
me-1448_1_task-force

- http://www.nytimes.com/1990/09/22/us/police-criti-cized-in-san-diego

- http://articles.latimes.com/1990-06-28/news/
mn-644_1_san-diego-police

- http://articles.latimes.com/1993-01-11/entertainment/
ca-1042_1_wake-upcall-latimes

- http://articles.latimes.com/1992-02-21/local/
me-2474_1_san-diego-police

- http://articles.latimes.com/1992-10-27/local/me-716_1_
sexual-assault

- http://articles.latimes.com/1991-04-27/local/me-449_1_
task-force

- http://articles.latimes.com/1992-03-01/local/
me-5525_1_donna-gentile

- http://articles.latimes.com/1990-09-26/local/me-951_1_
police-officers

- http://articles.latimes.com/1990-09-25/local/me-975_1_
task-force

- https://www.sandiegoreader.com/news/2013/nov/18/
ticker-sdpd-vice-chief-kenneth-moller-succumbs-can/

- www.sdnews.com

- https://dec17philly.com/there-really-are-people-who-dont-care-when-prostitutes-are-victims-of-hate-crimes-beaten-raped-and-murdered-no-matter-what-you-think-about-sex-workers-and-the-politics-surrounding-them-sex-w/

- San Diego Union Tribune: www.sandiegouniontribune.
com

- Tabor Home: www.tabor.org

- https://www.voiceamerica.com/promo/episode/76517

- http://www.renewamerica.com/columns/miles/150323

- http://www.imdb.com/title/tt2635976/

- http://www.democraticunderground.com/125511729

- http://www.worldcat.org/title/murder-of-donna-
gentile-san-diego-policing and prostitution

- https://www.sdsheriff.net/detentionfacilities/lcdrf.html

- http://web.sdcaa.com/Property-Management/Hanken,-
Cono,-Assad-Co-319

- https://www.sandiegocounty.gov/me/

- https://www.countyoffice.org/ca-san-diego-county-
medical-coroner/w

- http://obrag.org/?p=38172

- https://www.dailydot.com/irl/president-trump-sesta-
fosta-law/

- https://sandiegoreader.com/news/1991/oct/10/cover-
karen-wilkening

- https://www.voiceofsandiego.org/topics/news/
from-police-chief-to-recluse-catching-up-with-norm-
stamper/

- https://www.voiceofsandiego.org/topics/public-safety/
why-el-cajon-blvd-is-a-prostitution-hotspot/

- https://deborahsmall.wordpress.com/projects/public-art/4958-2/

- https://livestream.com/palomarcollegetv/PEDFall-l2013JerryLimberg/videos/32458505

- Professor Jerry Limberg: https://www.youtube.com/watch?v=HU6qh8PsUoo&t=324s

- http://articles.latimes.com/1985-07-06/local/me-9506_1_donna-gentile

- http://articles.latimes.com/1985-07-11/local/me-8538_1_probation-officer

- www.buckscountycouriertimes.com

- NHI: No Humans Involved Exhibition Artists: Deborah Small, Scott Kessler, Elizabeth Sisco, Carla Kirkwood, & Louis Hock http://www.LouisHock.info/

- Killing Women Book: Annette Burfort and Susan Lord

- "I'm in There! I'm one of the Women in That Picture!" Margot Leigh Butler

- Horse Nation Book: Theresa Tsimmu Martino

- The Love Poems of Rumi Book: Nader Khalili

- Cross Country Evil Book: Tom Basinski

- Breaking Rank Book: Norm Stamper: The Dark Side of American Policing

- Cop to Call Girl Book: Norma Jean Almodovar

- Carol Leigh: http://www.bayswan.org/leigh_bio.html

- Margo St James: Founder of the Prostitution Rights Movement. COYOTE and St. James Infirmary Clinic

- Dr. Annie Sprinkle: Annual International Day Dec 17 "End Violence Against Sexworkers"

- Norma Jean Almodovar: Police, Prostitution, Politics

- http://www.agjohnson.us/

- http://www.agjohnson.us/essays/silence/

- http://articles.latimes.com/1991-09-17/local/me-2674_1_task-force

- http://forensicfiles.wikia.com/wiki/Ronald_Porter

- http://articles.latimes.com/1992-09-23/local/me-1080_1_attempted-murder (Ronald Porter)

- https://gerardtomkophotography.shootproof.com/

- https://metoomvmt.org/

- https://sexualpolitixxx.blog/2018/11/04/newsday-follow-up-on-missing-pa-prostitute-corinna-slusser-of-bloomsburg/

- http://www.iswface.org/whowillrescueus.html

- http://www.coyotela.org/

- http://iswface.org/

- Phila Inquirer, Kathy Boccella: http://www.philly.com/philly/news/pennsylvania/philadelphia/sex-workers-victimized-by-violence-remembered-at-philadelphia-vigil-20171217.html

- https://www.youtube.com/watch?v=lIG-55tNbJM (90 women killed by Gary Ridgway)

- https://en.wikipedia.org/wiki/Gary_Ridgway

- http://articles.latimes.com/1992-02-25/entertainment/

ca-2595_1_public-art

- NHI Book: https://www.amazon.com/NHI-Humans-Involved-Deborah-Small/dp/B0015KKHWK

- copyrightland.net/killing-women/i-m-in-there-i-m-one-of-the-women-in-that-picture.htm

- https://en.wikipedia.org/wiki/Prostitution

- https://legal-dictionary.thefreedictionary.com/Police+Corruption+and+Misconduct

- Maxine Doogan:https://www.latimes.com/opinion/endorsements/la-ed-end-prop35-20121010-story.html

- Maxine Doogan: https://www.youtube.com/watch?v=F3t6WN4479Y

- Donna Gentile: https://dec17philly.com/2016/11/20/in-memory-of-philly-native-donna-gentile/

- San Diego Medical Examiner: https://www.sandiego-county.gov/me/

- Why Cops Get with Prostitutes, Norma Jean Almodovar: https://www.youtube.com/watch?v=piTBoNrIOxg

- Norma Jean Almodovar: https://en.wikipedia.org/wiki/Norma_Jean_Almodovar

- CBS8 San Diego, Dec. 2018: http://www.cbs8.com/clip/14714808/anita-defrancesco-author-of-the-donna-gentile-story

- CBS8 San Diego, Dec. 2018: David Gotfredson: http://www.cbs8.com/story/39645511/new-book-details-evidence-in-unsolved-1985-murder-of-donna-gentile

Further Information

- Children of the Night, Dr. Lois Lee: https://www.childrenofthenight.org/

- WOAR: https://www.woar.org/

- Melanie Dante: https://dec17philly.com/category/activism-advocacy-allies/

- Melanie Dante-Wikidelphia

- http://wikidelphia.org/wiki/Melanie_Dante

- Melanie Dante: www.BDC-Lancaster.net

- International Day Dec 17 "End Violence Against Sexworkers http://www.december17.org/

- Dr. Timaree Leigh Schmit, Widener University, can be found: https://sexwithtimaree.com/

- Dr. Robin Lowey Phila: https://drlowey.com/

- https://dec17philly.com/2016/11/20/in-memory-of-philly-native-donna-gentile/

- Norma Jean Almodovar, Founder: International Sex Work Foundation For Art Culture &Education in Los-Angeles: http://www.iswface.org/

- Norma Jean Almodovar: Coyote LA: http://www.coyotela.org/

- Norma Jean Almodovar:http://www.normajeansgifts.com/

- Norma Jean Almodovar:http://www.normajeanalmodovar.com/

- Norma Jean Almodovar: http://www.policeprostitutionandpolitics.com/

- Maxine Doogan, Founder: Sex Workers and Erotic Service Providers Legal, Educational: https://esplerp.org/
- The Red Umbrella Project: https://www.redumbrellaproject.org/
- The Global Alliance Against Traffic in Women (GAATW): http://www.gaatw.org
- https://dec17philly.com/2016/11/06/coming-out-under-the-red-umbrella/
- www.compassionatefriends.org
- http://www.waygay.org/
- www.crimewatchers.net
- www.victimsofcrime.org
- Black Coalition Fights Back: http://www.blackcoalitionfightingbackserialmurders.net/
- National Coalition Against Domestic Violence: http://ncadv.org/
- Project Home, Sister Mary Scullion: https://projecthome.org/
- Safehouse: https://www.safehousephilly.org/ (Rendell)
- www.njhumantrafficking.org
- www.ahomefordawn.org
- www.tabor.org
- www.osaphilly.org
- https://thedumas.com/
- Scarlet Road Documentary with Touching Base: http://

www.scarletroad.com.au/about/

- Sex Worker Outreach Project (SWOP) USA: www.new. swopusa.org

- SAFE: https://projectsafephilly.org/tag/advocacy/

- The Rape Foundation: www.therapefoundation.org

- http://iamatreasure.com/

- http://myfriendsplace.org/

- https://www.covenanthouse.org/

- www.survivorsagainstsestafosta.org

- Dr. Annie Sprinkle:www.anniesprinkle.org

- http://anitadefrancesco.com/wp-content/ uploads/2018/02/VIOLENCE-SEX-DONNA-GENTILE-12-17-17.mp3

- http://anitadefrancesco.com/wp-content/ uploads/2017/05/in-memoriam-donna-gentile-anita-defrancesco.mp3

- Dr. Susan Kaye: http://www.instituteformindbody-therapy.org/

- Bond Wright: http://wrightbodymind.com/

- Tantra Wisdom:www.tantrawisdom.com

- Sacred Sexual Healing For Women: http://amritagrace. com/

- Sexual Empowerment For Women https://amyjo-goddard.com/

- Ava Cadell Loveology University: https://www.loveuniv. com/

- American Association of Sexuality Educators, Therapists:https://www.aasect.org/

- Professor Jerry Kathleen Limberg: San Diego California State College Professor 2012 YouTube Documentary, The Murder of Donna Gentlie

- Mariska Hagitay Criminal Minds Actor/Founder: http://www.joyfulheartfoundation.org/

- Halle Berry: https://jenesse.org/

- Moment of Truth Movie: Why My Daughter? Diana Moffitt Story

- Changeling Movie starring Angelina Jolie

- Monster Movie starring Charlize Theron

- Killing Women Book: By Annette Burfoot & Susan Lord

- Sexual Personae Book: Camille Paglia

- Critical Condition Book: Women on the Edge of Violence, Amy Scholder

- The Slave Across the Street Book: Theresa Flores

- Cop to Call Girl Book: Norma Jean Almodovar

- The Function of the Orgasm Book: https://en.wikipedia.org/wiki/Wilhelm_Reich

- The Voice of the Body Book: https://en.wikipedia.org/wiki/Alexander_Lowen

- No Human Involved Book: By Sheron Linn

- https://www.themarshallproject.org/

- Lou Boxer, True Crime Books Noircon: https://www.noircon.com/

- https://espu-ca.org/
- Wrongly Accused Book: Glesty Waters
- Glesty Waters : Linkedin
- Larry Avrech: Linkedin www.whokilleddonnagentile.com
- Mike Kiger, PI: http://www.missinginc.com/index.htm
- JJ McKeever: www.jjwriting-consulting.com
- Di Freeze: www.freezetimemedia.com
- Jonathan Borowko Illustration Artist: https://www.linkedin.com/in/jonathanborowko/
- Sexploratorium Education: https://passionalboutique.wordpress.com/sexploratorium/
- Kink Sex Education: https://www.kinkshoppe.com/
- Pleasure Chest Sex Education: https://www.thepleasurechest.com/
- Peter Zales: http://affordableoffset.com/
- Nathan Kuruna: Multimedia: http://nathankuruna.com/
- JPac Productions: Videography, Multimedia: http://www.jpacproductions.com/
- Johnny "Lemuria" Robinson: Multimedia: http://johnnylemuria.com/
- Facebook: The Donna Gentile Story
- www.TheDonnaGentileStory.com

Rosey Publishing

More Books

Made in the USA
San Bernardino, CA
20 June 2019